PHLEGON OF TRALLES' BOOK OF MARVELS

EXETER STUDIES IN HISTORY

General Editors: Jonathan Barry, Tim Rees and T.P. Wiseman

Phlegon of Tralles' Book of Marvels

Translated with an Introduction
and Commentary by

William Hansen

ἔνια δ' ὑπερβολὴν ἔχει κατὰ τόνδε τὸν κόσμον.
Φιλόδημος, Περὶ σημειώσεων

Some things in this universe are extraordinary.
Philodemos, *On Signs*

UNIVERSITY
of
EXETER
PRESS

First published in 1996 by
University of Exeter Press
Reed Hall, Streatham Drive
Exeter, Devon EX4 4QR
UK
www.exeterpress.co.uk

Printed digitally since 2010

British Library Cataloguing in Publication Data
A catalogue record for this book is
available from the British Library

ISBN 978 0 85989 425 8

Typeset in 11/13pt Sabon by
Greenshires Icon, Exeter

Printed and bound by CPI Group (UK) Ltd, Croydon, CR0 4YY

For my wife Mary Beth,
whose love and support I have enjoyed
during the writing of this book.

Contents

Preface

Phlegon's *Book of Marvels* probably reflects the interests and tastes of ordinary readers of its time, the second century of our era. A compendium of wondrous and bizarre phenomena, it is the earliest surviving work of pure sensationalism in Western literature. It is of particular interest to cultural historians in providing so clear an example of a particular kind of popular literature, and to folklorists in illustrating contemporary oral narrative and folk belief. Phlegon's method of work also incorporates fascinating documentary material such as Sibylline oracles and census data.

I have written the commentary with the general reader as well as the classical scholar in mind and I hope that the translation, the first into any modern language, and the commentary will be of interest to both.

For help of various kinds I happily express my debt and gratitude to John Bancroft, Cynthia Bannon, Matthew Christ, Henry Glassie, Mary Beth Hannah-Hansen, Inge Hansen, Julene Hoffman, Eleanor Winsor Leach, Gregory Schrempp, Alex Scobie, Josep Sobrer, and T.P. Wiseman.

Abbreviations and Select Bibliography

AT   Antti Aarne and Stith Thompson, *The Types of the Folktale: A Classification and Bibliography*, FF Communications 184, Helsinki 1961.

Bird   S. Elizabeth Bird, *For Enquiring Minds: A Cultural Study of Supermarket Tabloids*, Knoxville 1992.

Barbin   Herculine Barbin, *Herculine Barbin: Being the Recently Discovered Memoirs of a Nineteenth-Century French Hermaphrodite*, introd. Michel Foucault, trans. Richard McDougall, New York 1980.

Brisson 1976   Luc Brisson, *Le mythe de Tirésias: Essai d'analyse structurale*, Leiden 1976.

Brisson 1978   Luc Brisson, 'Aspects politiques de la bisexualité: L'histoire de Polycrite', in *Hommages à Maarten J. Vermaseren*, Margreet B. de Boer and T.A. Edridge (eds), Édition spéciale des Études préliminaires aux religions orientales dans l'empire romain 68, Leiden 1978, 1: 80–122.

Burkert   Walter Burkert, *Greek Religion*, trans. John
                   Raffan, Cambridge MA 1985.

Christ   Wilhelm von Christ, *Geschichte der griechis-
                   chen Litteratur*, umgearbeitet von Wilhelm
                   Schmid und Otto Stählin, 6th edn, 2 vols,
                   Munich 1920–24.

Delcourt 1938   Marie Delcourt, *Stérilités mystérieuses et
                   naissances maléfiques dans l'antiquité clas-
                   sique*, Liège and Paris 1938.

den Boer   W. den Boer, *Private Morality in Greece and
                   Rome: Some Historical Aspects*, Mnemosyne
                   Suppl. 57, Leiden 1979.

Diels   Hermann Diels, *Sibyllinische Blätter*, Berlin
                   1890.

Doria   Luisa Breglia Pulci Doria, *Oracoli Sibillini tra
                   Rituali e Propaganda: Studi su Flegonte di
                   Tralles*, Naples 1983.

EM   *Enzyklopädie des Märchens: Handwörter-
                   buch zur historischen und vergleichenden
                   Erzählforschung*, Kurt Ranke et al. (eds),
                   Berlin and New York 1977 ff.

Ferguson   John Ferguson, *Bibliographical Notes on
                   Histories of Inventions and Books of Secrets*,
                   2 vols, London 1959.

FGH   Felix Jacoby (ed.), *Die Fragmente der
                   griechischen Historiker*, 3 vols in 14, Berlin
                   and Leiden 1923–58.

Finley and Pleket M.I. Finley and H.W. Pleket, *The Olympic
                   Games: The First Thousand Years*, London
                   1976.

Fontenrose	Joseph Fontenrose, *The Delphic Oracle: its Responses and Operations, with a Catalogue of Responses*, Berkeley and Los Angeles 1978.
Forbes Irving	P.M.C. Forbes Irving, *Metamorphosis in Greek Myths*, Oxford 1990.
Frank	Eva Frank, 'Phlegon', in RE 20: 261–64.
Gabba 1975	Emilio Gabba, 'P. Cornelio Scipione Africano e la leggenda', *Athenaeum* 53, 1975, 3–17.
Gabba 1981	Emilio Gabba, 'True History and False History in Classical Antiquity', *Journal of Roman Studies* 71, 1981, 50–62.
Gantz	Timothy Gantz, *Early Greek Myth: A Guide to Literary and Artistic Sources*, Baltimore and London 1993.
Garland	Robert Garland, *The Eye of the Beholder: Deformity and Disability in the Graeco–Roman World*, Ithaca 1995.
Gauger	Jörg-Dieter Gauger, 'Phlegon von Tralleis, mirab. III: Zu einem Dokument geistigen Widerstandes gegen Rom', *Chiron* 10, 1980, 225–61.
Giannini 1963	Alessandro Giannini, 'Studi sulla paradossografia greca I. Da Omero a Callimaco: motivi e forme del meraviglioso', *Istituto Lombardo (Rend. Lett.)* 97, 1963, 247–66.
Giannini 1964	Alessandro Giannini, 'Studi sulla paradossografia greca II. Da Callimaco all'età imperiale: la letteratura paradossografica', *Acme* 17, 1964, 99–140.

Giannini 1965   Alexander   Giannini   (ed.),   *Paradoxo-*
                  graphorum Graecorum Reliquiae, Milan
                  1965.

Hansen 1980   William Hansen, 'An Ancient Greek Ghost
                  Story', in *Folklore on Two Continents: Essays
                  in Honor of Linda Dégh*, Nikolai Burlakoff
                  and Carl Lindahl (eds), Bloomington IN
                  1980, 71–77.

Hansen 1989   William Hansen, 'Contextualizing the Story
                  of Philinnion', *Midwestern Folklore* 15,
                  1989, 101–8.

Harris   H.A. Harris, *Greek Athletes and Athletics*,
                  Bloomington IN and London 1966.

Holleaux   Maurice Holleaux, 'Sur un passage de
                  Phlégon de Tralles', *Revue de Philologie* 4,
                  1930, 305–09, repr. with a few additions: 'Sur
                  une passage de Phlégon de Tralles', *Études
                  d'épigraphie et d'histoire grecques* 5, 1957,
                  244–48.

Janda   Jan Janda, 'D'Antisthène, auteur des
                  Successions des philosophes', *Listy Filologické*
                  89, 1966, 341–64.

Jones and   Ann Rosalind Jones and Peter Stallybrass,
Stallybrass   'Fetishizing Gender: Constructing the
                  Hermaphrodite in Renaissance Europe', in
                  *Bodyguards: The Cultural Politics of Gender
                  Ambiguity*, Julia Epstein and Kristina Straub
                  (eds), New York and London 1991, 80–111.

Klein   Josef Klein, 'Epigraphisch-antiquarische
                  Analekten', *RhM* 33, 1878, 128–37.

Krappe	A.H. Krappe, 'Teiresias and the Snakes', *American Journal of Philology* 49, 1928, 267–75.
Mac.	*De Macrobiis* = Περὶ Μακροβίων = *Long-Lived Persons.*
MacBain	Bruce MacBain, *Prodigy and Expiation: A Study in Religion and Politics in Republican Rome*, Collection Latomus 177, Brussels 1982.
Martelli	Fabio Martelli, 'Ancora in margine ad un frammento di Antistene', *Rivista Storica dell' Antichità* 12, 1982, 251–60.
Mesk	Josef Mesk, 'Über Phlegons Mirabilia I–III', *Philologus* 80, 1925, 298–311.
Miller	Stephen G. Miller, *Arete: Greek Sports from Ancient Sources*, 2nd edn, Berkeley, Los Angeles, Oxford 1991.
Mir.	*De Mirabilibus* = Περὶ Θαυμασίων = *Book of Marvels.*
Morel	Willy Morel, 'Zum Text des Phlegon von Tralles', *Philologische Wochenschrift* 54, 1934, 171–76.
Nicolet	C. Nicolet, *The World of the Citizen in Republican Rome*, trans. P.S. Falla, London 1980.
Ol.	*Olympiades* = Ὀλυμπιάδες = *Olympiads.*
Park and Daston	Katharine Park and Lorraine J. Daston, 'Unnatural Conceptions: The Study of Monsters in Sixteenth- and Seventeenth-Century France and England,' *Past and Present* 92, 1981, 20–54.

Parke H.W. Parke. *Sibyls and Sibylline Prophecy in Classical Antiquity*, B.C. McGing (ed.), Croom Helm Classical Studies, London and New York 1988.

Parke and Wormell H.W. Parke and D.E.W. Wormell. *The Delphic Oracle*, 2 vols, Oxford 1956.

Peretti Aurelio Peretti, 'Una storia di fantasmi oracolanti', *Studi classici e orientali* 33, 1983, 39–81.

Pighi Ioannes Baptista Pighi, *De Ludis Saecularibus Populi Romani Quiritium*, Milan 1941.

Pilgrim David Pilgrim, *Human Oddities: An Exploratory Study*, Notre Dame IN 1984.

Potter D.S. Potter, *Prophecy and History in the Crisis of the Roman Empire: A Historical Commentary on the Thirteenth Sibylline Oracle*, Oxford 1990.

RE *Paulys Real-Encyclopädie der classischen Altertumswissenschaft*, Georg Wissowa (ed.), Stuttgart 1894 ff.

RhM *Rheinisches Museum für Philologie*

Robinson Rachel S. Robinson, *Sources for the History of Greek Athletics In English Translation*, Cincinnati 1955.

Rohde Erwin Rohde, 'Zu den Mirabilia des Phlegon', *RhM* N.F. 32, 1877, 331–39.

Roscher W.H. Roscher (ed.), *Lexikon der griechischen und römischen Mythologie*, 7 vols, Leipzig 1884–86.

Schenda Rudolf Schenda, *Die französische Prodigien-literatur in der zweiten Hälfte des 16. Jahrhunderts*, Munich 1961.

Schulze Wilhelm Schulze, *Zur Geschichte Lateinischer Eigennamen*, 2nd edn, Berlin/Zürich, Dublin 1966.

Spectacles Sportifs *Spectacles Sportifs et Scéniques dans le Monde Étrusco-Italique*. Actes de la table ronde organisée par l'Équipe de recherches étrusco-italiques de l'UMR 126, CNRS, Paris, et l'École française de Rome, Rome 1993.

Swahn Jan-Öjvind Swahn, *The Tale of Cupid and Pyche: Aarne-Thompson 425 and 428*, Lund 1955.

Thompson Stith Thompson, *A Motif-Index of Folk-Literature: A Classification of Narrative Elements in Folktales, Ballads, Myths, Fables, Mediaeval Romances, Exempla, Fabliaux, Jest-Books and Local Legends*, Rev. edn, 6 vols, Bloomington IN 1955.

Wachsmuth Curt Wachsmuth, *Einleitung in das Studium der alten Geschichte*, Leipzig 1895.

Weber Wilhelm Weber, *Untersuchungen zur Geschichte des Kaisers Hadrianus*, Leipzig 1907.

Wendland 1911a Paul Wendland, 'Antike Geister- und Gespenstergeschichten', in *Festschrift zur Jahrhunderfeier der Universität zu Breslau im Namen der Schlesischen Gesellschaft für Volkskunde*, Theodor Siebs (ed.), Breslau 1911, 9–32.

Wendland 1911b   Paul Wendland, *De Fabellis Antiquis earumque ad Christianos Propagatione*, Göttingen 1911.

West   M.L. West (ed.), *Hesiod: Works and Days*, Oxford 1978.

Winkler   Jack Winkler, 'Lollianos and the Desperadoes', *Journal of Hellenic Studies* 100, 1980, 155–81.

Wittkower   Rudolf Wittkower, 'Marvels of the East: A Study in the History of Monsters', *Journal of the Warburg and Courtauld Institutes* 5, 1942, 159–97.

Young   Mark C. Young, (ed.), *The Guinness Book of Records 1995*, New York 1994.

Ziegler   Konrat Ziegler, 'Paradoxographoi', in *RE* 18: 1137–66.

1

Introduction

Phlegon was a Greek freedman of the Emperor Hadrian (AD 117–38) who served on the emperor's staff. References in his writings show a familiarity with events and persons of the imperial court: he mentions the preserved body of a centaur that was kept in the emperor's storehouse (*Mir.* 35); says that he saw a certain extraordinary man on the occasion of his being shown to the emperor (*Mac.* 97); and dedicates one of his books, *Olympiads*, to a certain Alkibiades, also a member of the imperial staff (Photios *Bibl.* 97.2 = *FGH* 257 T 3). He was sufficiently well known to become entangled in malicious gossip that circulated about the emperor. It was said that certain books ostensibly authored by Phlegon had really been written by the emperor, Hadrian allegedly being so desirous of renown that he wrote essays about himself and had his educated freedmen publish them under their own names (*Script. Hist. Aug.* 1.16.1). Although no one believes this accusation, at least nowadays, the gossip suggests that among literary freedman attached to the emperor Phlegon's name came readily to mind. It may also be relevant that Greeks from Tralles (the Roman spelling of Tralleis, Phlegon's hometown in Caria in Asia Minor) and elsewhere are mentioned contemptuously by the Roman satirist Juvenal as contributing to the swarm of quick witted and ambitious Greeks who, to his dismay, had been gaining admittance in increasing numbers to the finest households in Rome (*Sat.* 3.70). In short, Phlegon was experienced in both Greek and Roman ways, including the imperial court, and was known as a writer. For further information on Phlegon's life and career generally, see Frank.

The Book of Marvels

Phlegon authored several books, of which the most remarkable is his *Book of Marvels* (Περὶ Θαυμασίων), a compilation of wondrous events and facts. A sample of its themes will give a fair idea of its nature: a dead girl carries on an affair, a father eats his own son; a maiden changes sex from female to male on her wedding day; a child is born with the head of the Egyptian god Anubis, a live centaur is captured; girls in a certain city give birth at seven years of age; bones of giant beings are discovered, and so on. The extent to which Phlegon's work is an ancient predecessor of the tabloids of today is a question that readily suggests itself, and I shall return to it below.

The *Book of Marvels* belongs to a genre of writing for which the ancients themselves possessed no special label, and which classical scholars call paradoxography 'writing about marvels', a term introduced in the early nineteenth century by Antonius Westermann, the editor of a collection of Greek writers on wonders (Westermann (ed.), Παραδοξογράφοι: *Scriptores Rerum Mirabilium Graeci*, Brunsvigae and Londini 1839). As an independent genre of writing paradoxography seems to have come into being at the confluence of two trends in Greek literature. One was an interest in the wondrous. Of course, marvels appear throughout ancient Greek literature from the works of Homer and Hesiod onward, but in the course of time the element of the wondrous claimed an increasing role, and beginning in the late fifth century BC fabulous histories, ethnographies and travel accounts were produced in increasing numbers (Wittkower 1942, Gabba 1981, Garland 1995, 159–77). A second trend was a fashion for compilations. From the fourth century BC onwards published collections of different sorts began to appear, such as the collection of Aesopic fables made by Demetrios of Phaleron, compilations of wit in the form of jokebooks, and in particular gatherings of ethnographic, biological and other data made by Peripatetic philosophers for the purpose of study and research. Collections of such information by Aristotle's successors reveal a growing enjoyment in remarkable information for its own sake, especially rarities, abnormalities and marvels of nature.

Paradoxography as a special form of literature arose in the early Hellenistic period when for the first time authors composed literary works that were devoted exclusively to the element of the marvellous. The founder of the genre was probably the poet and scholar Kallimachos of Cyrene (c.305–240 BC), who wrote the oldest work of independent paradoxography of which we have any record. Its full title was *A Collection of Wonders from the Entire Earth Arranged by Locality* (Θαυμάτων τῶν εἰς ἅπασαν τὴν γῆν κατὰ τόπους συναγωγή). Although Kallimachos's composition does not survive, it was drawn upon by subsequent paradoxographers, so that we can form a good idea of its contents and its organization, which was geographical. Different sections were devoted to marvels in Greece, Thrace, Italy, Africa and Asia, and topics included wondrous waters (rivers, springs, lakes), animals, plants, localities, stones and fire.

Kallimachos' work found many imitators. More than twenty Greek paradoxographers were active between the third century BC and the third century AD, together with many other authors whose writings were connected in some way with paradoxography. Although most of the books of the paradoxographers are known to us only in fragments or by allusion, seven survive more or less entire. They are *A Collection of Marvellous Researches* ('Ιστοριῶν παραδόξων συναγωγή) by Antigonos of Karystos, *Wondrous Researches* ('Ιστορίαι Θαυμάσιαι) by Apollonios, *On Marvels* (Περὶ Θαυμασίων)—rendered here as *Book of Marvels*—by Phlegon of Tralles and four works of unknown authorship: *On Wondrous Reports* (Περὶ Θαυμασίων ἀκουσμάτων) by pseudo-Aristotle and the compilations made by the so-called Florentine paradoxographer, the Vatican paradoxographer, and the Palatine paradoxographer, whose authors and original titles are uncertain. Paradoxography found a niche in Roman literature as well. The late-republican scholar Marcus Terentius Varro authored a book *De Admirandis* 'On Marvels', and Cicero composed a similar work (Pliny *NH* 31.8.12, 31.28.51), although neither has survived. However, the encyclopedic *Natural History* of the Elder Pliny includes virtually every topic that was dear to the paradoxographers, except that Pliny does not select for wondrous phenomena alone but intermingles the wondrous and the ordinary. The passion for paradoxography was expressed sporadically in other Greek and Roman authors of the time, notably in the novelists, and of course material wonders of many kinds were on public display, especially in temples.

For the texts of the Greek paradoxographers see Giannini (1965) and on paradoxography in general see Ziegler, Giannini (1963, 1964). On the passion for the strange and exotic during the Hadrianic age see Alex Scobie, *Aspects of the Ancient Romance and its Heritage: Essays on Apuleius, Petronius, and the Greek Romances*, Meisenheim am Glan, (1969) 43–54; on Apuleius and paradoxography see H.J. Mason, 'Fabula Graecanica: Apuleius and his Greek Sources', in *Aspects of Apuleius' Golden Ass*, B.L. Hijmans, Jr and R. Th. van der Paardt (eds), (Groningen 1978) 8, and John J. Winkler, *Auctor and Actor: A Narratological Reading of Apuleius's 'The Golden Ass'*, (Berkeley 1985), 256 ff.; and on paradoxography in the Greek novelists see Hans Rommel, *Die naturwissenschaftlich-paradoxographischen Exkurse bei Philostratos, Heliodoros und Achilleus Tatios*, (Stuttgart 1923).

Antigonos (fl. 240 BC) was a younger contemporary of Kallimachos, and his work in its present form (the last page of the text has been lost) is a compilation of 173 brief entries. There is no preface, so that the work simply begins with its first entry. Some principles of organization are discernible: Chapters 1–108 concern zoology; 109–118 deal with human physiology; 119–28 are mostly about places with dangerous exhalations; and 129–73 are excerpts from Kallimachos dealing with a variety of wonders, mostly waters (129–65). So Antigonos replaces Kallimachos's geographical deployment with a topical arrangement. He generally mentions his sources, and in regard to these the work falls into five parts. Section I consists of excerpts drawn from a variety of authors, acting as a kind of introduction to Sections II and III, which are drawn from Aristotle, Section IV consists of excerpts drawn from miscellaneous authors, and Section V is another long series of excerpts from a single author, in this case Kallimachos. The following entries are typical:

> 14 Theopompos says that in Chalkideis in Thrace there is a certain place having the peculiarity that any animal that enters it exits again unharmed, except for dung-beetles, which do not escape but turn around in a circle and die on the spot. For this reason the place is called Kantharolethron ('Dung-Beetle-Death').

> 22 The bat is the only bird that has teeth, breasts, and milk. Aristotle says that seals and whales also have milk, and he records something even more amazing than this, which is that on Lemnos so much milk was milked from a he-goat that cheese was made from it.

> 122 It is reported that on the island of Leuke no bird is able to fly over the temple of Achilleus.

The work of Apollonios (second century BC?) is a collection of fifty-one entries, mostly quite brief. The first part (1–6) features legendary traditions about men of wondrous powers or to whom something wondrous befell, such as Epimenides of Crete, the Rip van Winkle of ancient Greek tradition. The rest (7–51) concern the natural world, mostly botany, zoology and human biology, together with a few items devoted to marvellous springs, rocks and ethnography, all organized according to no obvious principle. An apparent innovation of Apollonios is his inclusion of material concerning human beings. He usually gives the author and work from which he excerpts, for example:

1 It is said that Epimenides of Crete was sent by his father and uncles to their farm to bring a sheep back to town. When night overtook him he left the path and slept for fifty-seven years according to many authorities, including Theopompos in his historical treatise that deals with marvels by locality. In the meantime the members of Epimenides's household died, and when he awoke from his sleep he looked for the sheep he had been sent to bring, and not finding it he went to the farm—he assumed that he had awoken on the same day on which he had fallen asleep—but he found that the farm was sold and the equipment was changed. Returning to town he went to his own house, where he learned what had happened, including the events during the time when he was missing. The Cretans, according to Theopompos, say that he died after a lifetime of 150 years. Many other marvellous things are also told about this man.

14 Phylarchos says in the eighth book of his historical treatise that in the Arabian Gulf there is a spring of water and if a man rubs his feet with it his genitals immediately become extremely erect. Some persons' genitals do not contract again at all, whereas others' do return to normal size but only after great suffering and treatment.

23 It is amazing that the sun tans us whereas fire does not do so at all, and that a diamond does not become hot when it is placed over fire, and that a magnet attracts during the daytime whereas at night it attracts less or not at all.

24 Eudoxos of Rhodes says that there is a people in Celtic territory who see not during the daytime but at night.

The compilation *On Wondrous Reports* (third century BC to sixth century AD?), which, since at least the second century AD has been attributed falsely to Aristotle, is known in a number of versions that differ in the arrangement of the material and in the number of entries. The largest version contains 178 items, but in all cases the collection is a patchwork made from a number of smaller compositions and so exhibits more than one principle of organization. Generally speaking the topics are animals (1–30), humans (31–32), fire (33–41), metals and the like (42–62), and animals again (63–77), after which the arrangement changes from topical to geographical (78–138) and then again to a mainly zoological theme (139–51), ending with a final miscellany of rivers, animals, and stones (152–78). Few attributions of source are given. The following is an example:

> 83 They say that no wolves, bears, snakes, and animals of this sort are born on Crete on account of the fact that Zeus was born on it.

Finally, the so-called Florentine, Vatican and Palatine paradoxographers made small collections featuring short excerpts. The Florentine (second century AD?) contains forty-three items concerning waters, the Vatican (second century AD?) had sixty-two items on various topics (animals, waters, ethnography, geology, mythological transformations, etc., grouped thematically to some extent), and the Palatine (third century AD?) twenty-one entries (the subjects are animals, waters, stones and medicinal plants, some in thematic clusters and some not). The authors cite many sources for their excerpts but frequently have them at second or third hand from earlier compilers, as often is the case in other paradoxographical compilations as well. A few samples follow:

> *Flor.* 1 A spring in Potniai near Thebes from which horses drink and become mad, as Isigonos says in the second book of his *Incredible Matters*.

> *Flor.* 3 A spring in India that ejects persons swimming in it onto the ground as though by a machine of war, as Ktesias reports.

> *Vat.* 26 Among the Krobyzoi it is customary to mourn for a newborn baby and congratulate a deceased person.

> *Vat.* 27 Among the Nasamones in Africa the custom is for the bride to have sexual intercourse with all the guests on the first

night and to receive gifts from them, and thereafter to have
sexual intercourse only with the groom.

Vat. 31 Teiresias the son of Eueres saw two snakes copulating
and killed them; instantly he became a woman, and not long
thereafter a man. Zeus and Hera took him as a judge of the
pleasure of women and men in sexual intercourse. He said
that women's pleasure was the greater.

Pal. 12 (1) Andronikos says that in a certain place in Spain
gems are found scattered about that are naturally polygonal.
Some are white, others the colour of wax, and they produce
gems like themselves. As an experiment I myself acquired one,
which in fact did bear for me, so that the report is not a lie.

As this survey illustrates, the format employed by the paradoxographers is that of the compilation. Excerpts, mostly brief, are
given one after the other, arranged by locality, source, theme,
with a mixture of these principles, or arbitrarily. Their prose style
is simple, rather than striving for effect, for interest lies in the
content, not in the exposition. The original topics of the genre
remain the favourites: the marvellous characteristics and properties of animals, plants, stones, waters, localities, fire—in other
words, wondrous natural phenomena, but the genre grew to
embrace other topics as well. Of these, the most notable is
amazing human beings, whether individuals, whole communities, or characters belonging to Greek mythological history,
although mythology, despite its fabulous content, never came to
play a major role in paradoxography, for the compilers were
attracted more to the wonders of the contemporary and near-
contemporary world than to prehistory.

Only rarely do the compilers show an interest in the analysis
or interpretation of their material, which they present, not to
illustrate general principles or to facilitate the discovery of new
knowledge, but solely for the pleasure of its immediate interest.
For this reason, perhaps, none of the works contains introductory or concluding remarks explaining the author's purpose or
philosophy or method, except for brief remarks with which

Antigonos (Chapters 26 and 60) occasionally prefaces internal sections of his work. The authors make no show of exercising critical judgment regarding what to admit into their collections and, inasmuch as their evident aim was the presentation of natural and human wonders in a light spirit rather than as data for scientific investigation, it is not likely that the veracity of their data mattered greatly either to them or to their readers. In fact, truth took second place to creating in the reader an enjoyable sensation of awe at the wonders of nature and culture. The authors give the overall impression that they relate their wonders in good faith.

Paradoxography has not been treated kindly by modern critics. The standard literary histories scarcely mention it, and when scholars do have occasion to refer to the genre, they give it poor reviews. It is 'a parasitic growth on the tree of historic and natural-scientific literature,' declares Wilhelm von Christ (2: 237). As a genre paradoxography is 'arid', 'a degeneration of the interest in the marvellous', a 'banalization of a taste that became a mass phenomenon', a 'purely collectionistic mania drained of religious concern or ethnographic curiosity', writes Alexander Giannini (1963: 248). That paradoxography 'consists of catalogues of all the most bizarre and unintelligible phenomena of nature' is the view of James Romm, *The Edges of the Earth in Ancient Thought*, Princeton (1992), 92.

Of course, if it is measured against the standard of scientific research or philosophic inquiry, paradoxography fails miserably, but it does so because it does not aspire to such lofty aims, for after all one could easily turn the standard around, asking how well scientific and philosophic treatises would fare as recreational reading. In truth paradoxography is not so much bad science and bad ethnography as it is entertaining reading with a flavour of learning. It is a kind of popular literature, writing that aims to be broadly accessible by making minimal demands on its readers by concerning itself more with content than with style and by entertaining rather than challenging. It is light reading that does not take itself very seriously. Popular literature has

greater appeal overall for the average consumer than for the
more discerning reader but can also function as recreational
reading for the latter; moreover, most readers probably manifest
different levels of discernment in different kinds of literature.

Rather than compare paradoxography with something to
which it is dissimilar, let us compare it with something to which it
is similar. A *paradoxon*, I suggest, resembles nothing so much as
an anecdote, that is, a brief narrative in oral or literary tradition
that allegedly recalls a memorable utterance, action or experience
of a named person on a particular occasion. For example:

> Asked by Dionysios why philosophers go to the doors of the
> wealthy but the wealthy no longer go to the doors of philoso-
> phers, he (Aristippos) said: 'Because the former know what
> they need whereas the latter do not' (Diogenes Laertios *Lives
> of the Philosophers* 2.69).
>
> When Krates saw an uneducated boy, he hit the boy's paeda-
> gogus (Quintilian *Inst. Orat.* 1.9.5).

Both anecdotes and *paradoxa* are brief statements focusing on
something memorable or remarkable. Both are related as though
true and presumably are enjoyed all the more because they may
be true, but in fact they are enjoyable whether they happen to be
true or not, and ultimately their historical or scientific veracity is
not crucial to their immediate effect as narratives.

Just as an anecdote purports to convey a remarkable moment
in the life of an interesting person—a moment that in fact may
never have happened or may not have happened quite so strikingly as it is crystallized in the anecdote, a moment that, literally
true or not, ideally captures something characteristic about the
protagonist—so also a *paradoxon* purports to convey a remarkable and interesting phenomenon of the world—a phenomenon
that may not be true or may not be wholly true as it is formu-
lated in the *paradoxon* but is striking and wondrous nevertheless.
Both are modest narrative forms but are capable of effectiveness
and artfulness in their own realms, so that each genre has

frequently been published in the form of collections. Just as it would be pointless to judge anecdotes as biography, which they may resemble but do not claim or aspire to be, it is pointless to judge paradoxography as science and ethnography.

On the ancient anecdote and related genres see William Hansen, 'Folklore', in *Civilization of the Ancient Mediterranean: Greece and Rome,* Michael Grant and Rachel Kitzinger (eds), New York 1988, 2: 1121–30; Ronald F. Hock and Edward N. O'Neal, *The Chreia in Ancient Rhetoric,* Atlanta 1986; and Clive Skidmore, *Practical Ethics for Roman Gentlemen: The Work of Valerius Maximus,* Exeter 1996. On the modern folkloristic study of the anecdote see Richard Bauman, *Story, Performance, and Event: Contextual Studies in Oral Narrative,* Cambridge 1986, 54–77.

Although Phlegon's compilation of thirty-five marvels is typical of the ancient paradoxographical tradition in some ways, it is quite atypical in others. The work takes the usual form of a series of wondrous items of information drawn largely from earlier authors, presented serially with or without documentation and with little editorial comment, and related for the most part in simple prose. Items are arranged thematically, as they are in some other paradoxographies (at least in part), and there is a logical progression in the arrangement of the thematic clusters. But the work shows little interest in topics of the natural world that traditionally dominate paradoxographical works and instead focuses almost exclusively upon human phenomena, and within this realm it dwells especially on the sensational, the grotesque and the bizarre: revenants, hermaphrodites, human oddities, giant bones, live centaurs and so on. My point is not that a fascination with such phenomena was unusual for persons in Phlegon's day for patently it was not, rather it is that sensationalistic wonders were not the usual stuff of ancient paradoxography. Moreover, Phlegon edits his materials far less than other paradoxographers do, with the result that individual items in his collection vary wildly in magnitude from as short as a single sentence to as long as several pages, including in some cases extensive documents that, instead of being summarized, are copied out word for word.

Presumably this choice of themes expresses the author's personal interest in human phenomena, just as other compilers differ among themselves in their fondness for one or another aspect of nature and culture. It is possible that he did not set out in the first place to make a collection of wonders but made one because he already had accumulated sufficient data, materials that he had previously collected for a different work, *Olympiads* (see below, p.58); if so, the materials at hand may partially have determined the content of the collection instead of the genre's determining the selection of material. But I do not wish to take away from Phlegon's achievement, such as it is, by suggesting that his book somehow just happened into existence. Whatever his initial motive in scouting written and oral sources for items of sensationalistic import, he himself did the selecting, and accordingly he must be credited with producing the first compilation of sensationalistic literature in the Western world.

If paradoxography in general may remind modern readers of literary and journalistic features such as 'Ripley's Believe It Or Not', Phlegon is more likely to remind readers of the tabloids, weekly newspapers in tabloid form that are commonly displayed in supermarkets and contain *inter alia* bizarre and sensational human interest items that purport to be news. Here is a sample of headlines from the *Weekly World News* and the *Sun*:

'My Hubby Has Turned into a Frog, Sobs Wife. He croaks, catches flies and hops around the yard'

'Miracle Herb Melts Flab Away'

'Teen spins to death in a clothes dryer!'

'Amazing Rat Boy Has a 3-Foot Tail—*Exclusive Pix!*'

'Flying elephants drop cow pies on horrified crowd!'

'Amazing 2-Headed Baby is Proof of Reincarnation. One Head Speaks English—the Other Ancient Latin'

These outrageous items are not significantly different in kind from many of Phlegon's topics, which, if they bore headlines, might read as follows:

'Talking Head Foretells Future'

'Girl Changes into Man on Wedding Day'

'Skeletons of Giants Found in Cave'

'Child Born with Two Heads'

'Six-Year-Old Girls Give Birth'

'Live Centaur Captured'

and so on.

Of course there are differences as well. The modern tabloids are issued on a weekly schedule, whereas Phlegon authored a single book of sensationalism; the tabloids are inexpensive and sell in great numbers, whereas ancient books were costly and must have been published in very small numbers; the tabloids are lavishly illustrated, whereas Phlegon's book presumably was not illustrated at all; the tabloid journalists, who earn their living by writing, sometimes invent stories and documentation, since their aim is to sell as many papers as possible, whereas Phlegon derived no income from his book (no system of royalties existed in antiquity), did not invent anything at all, so far as one can tell, and provided honest (if also sometimes inadequate) documentation. Ultimately these differences are largely economic rather than literary in nature, reflecting the generally dissimilar conditions of writing and publishing in ancient and modern times and in particular the extremely commercial orientation of the modern tabloid press.

Economics apart, the sensationalism that is offered to the reader seems essentially to be of the same order. Both Phlegon and the supermarket tabloids feature astonishing, exciting and bizarre human interest stories that are set mostly in contemporary times, presented as true and recounted in a simple and direct fashion, so that, whether individual items are borrowed from other sources or invented out of whole cloth, their appeal to consumers must be similar. Some of Phlegon's themes are even favourites of today's tabloids: extremely young mothers, two-headed babies, hybrid offspring and, more generally, amazing finds and unexplained mysteries. Obviously there are readers who enjoy reading about strange and sensational events that are presented as true, however much the consumers believe what they read and however much they regard veracity as important.

The readership of the tabloids is by no means negligible, since sales of the top six tabloids run around ten million copies a week, with an estimated readership of fifty million (Bird 7). For the variety of readers and readings of supermarket tabloids see the interesting discussion of Bird (107–61). For example, some persons read the tabloids mostly for information, others to feel good about their own lives (their own problems seem less weighty in light of the greater problems faced by persons portrayed in the tabloid stories), others to be amused. Moreover, it is not uncommon for readers to take seriously one kind of tabloid feature (e.g., extra-terrestrials) and to disbelieve another (e.g., astrology). Concerning Phlegon's ancient readership we can only speculate, although, to judge from modern readers, there must have been more than one motive for reading the *Book of Marvels* and more than one kind of reader.

Sensationalism is not of course exclusive to the supermarket tabloids, which came into being in the 1980s, for it has enjoyed a long history in Western journalism (Bird 7–38) and literature. On supermarket tabloids see Bird's study, on the modern British tabloids see S.J. Taylor, *Shock! Horror! The Tabloids in Action,* London 1992, and on the journalistic fillers known in France as *faits divers* see Romi, *Histoire des Faits Divers,* Paris 1962, and Roland Barthes, 'Structure of the *Fait-Divers*', in *Critical Essays,* trans. Richard Howard, Evanston 1972, 185–95. Examples of sensationalism in early American newspapers and in English broadside ballads can be found respectively in Kenneth D. Nordin, 'The Entertaining Press: Sensationalism in 18th Century

Boston Newspapers', *Communication Research* 6, 1979, 295–320, and Hyder E. Rollins (ed.), *The Pack of Autolycus: or Strange and Terrible News of Ghosts, Apparitions, Monstrous Births, Showers of Wheat, Judgments of God, and other Prodigious and Fearful Happenings as told in Broadside Ballads of the Years 1624–1693*, Cambridge MA 1927. For natural wonders, especially so-called monsters (individual human oddities in Western nations as well as fabulous peoples in distant lands), in popular and learned works of the seventeenth century back to those of the Middle Ages see Louis B. Wright, *Middle-Class Culture in Elizabethan England*, Chapel Hill 1935, 561–72, Ferguson, Wittkower (vol. 1, pt 4), Schenda, and Park and Daston. Although the long history of sensationalism has yet to be written, its earliest surviving representative appears to be Phlegon's *Book of Marvels*.

As sources for his marvels Phlegon draws upon earlier authors, primarily historians and ethnographers but also the occasional poet, upon collections such as the paradoxographer Antigonos and the oracular poems that made up the famed Sibylline Books, and sometimes upon his own experience. His procedure is to report wonders in an apparently objective manner, buttressing their credibility in some cases by citing more than one example of the same kind of marvel, by declaring that the particular marvel is available for public inspection, or by claiming autopsy.

Unfortunately the initial pages of the *Book of Marvels* are lost because of damage to the single tenth-century manuscript in which the compilation, together with those of the paradoxographers Apollonios and Antigonos, survives, and it is uncertain how much of Phlegon's work is missing; in its present state the book begins in mid-sentence in the midst of a narrative about the return of a woman from the dead. Consequently, we do not know if Phlegon introduced his collection with a preface of some sort, although on the analogy of other paradoxographical works and of Phlegon's own *Long-Lived Persons* and *Olympiads*, it seems likely that the work had either very brief prefatory remarks or none at all, since paradoxographers were not much given to explanation.

The *Book of Marvels* has had a modest impact upon the scholarly and belletristic literature of later times. When the first printed Greek edition of Phlegon's *Book of Marvels* (as well as of the works of Apollonios and Antigonos) appeared in 1568, collections of natural marvels were fashionable in Europe, both in books of wonders and in cabinets of curiosities. Writers drew some material from ancient authors, especially from Pliny, whose widely-read *Natural History* had been available in printed editions since 1469, but also from other authors. The interest in Phlegon's *Book of Marvels* has focused mostly upon his ghost narratives. A number of sixteenth- and seventeenth-century writers of books on ghosts, demonology and other subjects regarded his stories as truthful accounts of actual events, as Phlegon himself did, and drew upon them as evidence for the nature of the supernatural or as sensational supernatural events. Frank (262) and Schenda (79) cite Delrio's *Disquisitiones Magicae* (1599), Petrus Lojerus's *Discours et Histoire des spectres* (1608), Johannes Praetorius's *Anthropodemus Plutonicus, das ist, Eine neue Weltbeschreibung von allerley wunderbaren Menschen* (1666), Remigius's *Daemonolatria* (1693) and others. In the realm of imaginative literature two notable authors have been inspired by the fragmentary but engagingly mysterious ghost narrative with which Phlegon's collection, at least in its present state, begins, for the story of Philinnion lies behind Goethe's vampire ballad, 'The Bride of Corinth' (see Appendix 2) as well as behind Washington Irving's short story, 'Adventure of the German Student'. The German poet apparently came upon Phlegon's story in the seventh chapter ('Von gestorbenen Leuten') of Praetorius' *Anthropodemus Plutonicus*; see James Boyd, *Notes to Goethe's Poems*, Oxford 1958, 2: 82–93, although his treatment of Phlegon (and indeed of everything Greek or Latin) is unreliable. For Washington Irving's tale, see his *Tales of a Traveller, by Geoffrey Crayon, Gent*, New York 1860, 57–64.

Other Writings

In addition to his *Book of Marvels* Phlegon authored several other works, including *A Description of Sicily, The Festivals of the Romans, A Topography of Rome, Long-Lived Persons,* and *Olympiads,* (*Suda* s.v. Φλέγων Τραλλιανός). From their titles it appears that they were all compilations of one sort or another, so that linearly-organized collections of information on different themes is probably a fair description of Phlegon's literary output. All these works however are lost except for the essay entitled *Long-Lived Persons* and some fragments of *Olympiads*. Since these two pieces have some interest and are not readily accessible in translation, I include them along with brief comments in the present volume.

Phlegon may have conceived his *Long-Lived Persons* and his *Book of Marvels* as being parts of a single work, for according to an entry in a Byzantine lexicon (*Suda* s.v. Φλέγων Τραλλιανός), Phlegon of Tralleis wrote a work, 'On Long-Lived Persons and Marvels' (Περὶ μακροβίων καὶ Θαυμασίων), and the tenth-century Greek manuscript in which the *Book of Marvels* and *Long-Lived Persons* are preserved contains a subscription at the end of Phlegon's text that reads: 'On Marvels and Long-Lived Persons, by Phlegon of Tralleis, freedman of the Emperor' (Φλέγοντος Τραλλιανοῦ ἀπελευθέρου Καίσαρος Περὶ Θαυμασίων καὶ μακροβίων). Although the lexicon and the manuscript do not agree on the sequence of the two works, the lexicon listing *Long-Lived Persons* as coming first and the manuscript listing it as coming second, as in fact it does in the manuscript, both represent them as somehow belonging together; however, the compilations themselves as we have them do not give the impression of being parts of a single, organic composition. Various solutions to this puzzle are imaginable, one being that Phlegon published the two compilations side-by-side as two small works dealing with the wondrous. Persons who live extraordinarily long lives are just as marvellous as, but at the opposite end of a continuum from, persons who appear to cycle through life's typical stages in a mere few years, a phenomenon that Phlegon illustrates in his *Book of Marvels* (Chapter 32–33). However these works were conceived originally, modern editors print them as separate compositions, and they are so treated here.

Phlegon's *Long-Lived Persons* consists primarily of classified lists of long-lived persons of various sorts, data that the author has obtained from several different sources, for example the records of the Roman census, anecdotal information about famous persons and Sibylline poetry. Organizing his material by age attained and moving from lower to higher, he begins with a list of persons who reached the age of 100 years, proceeds to persons who lived from 101 to 110 years and so on up to a person who attained the age of 150 years, after which he leaps to the instance of a certain Sibyl, or prophetess, whom he calculates to have lived around 1,000 years, whereupon the composition ends. The work has not survived intact, for there are obvious lacunae in the text as it has come down to us, but what is uncertain is whether, apart from the lacunae, we essentially have the whole essay or only a fragment of a larger work.

In *Long-Lived Persons* as in the *Book of Marvels* Phlegon seeks no causes and offers no explanations. Apparently his aim is simply to gather information and present it in a clear and organized fashion. The information itself he handles uncritically and without any scepticism, treating for example the Roman census and an oracular poem as equally reliable sources. *Long-Lived Persons* is not a scientific treatise, but Phlegon can hardly have conceived of it as entertaining reading either, for how amusing can it be to read the names of sixty-eight obscure persons who have attained the age of one hundred? For as in the *Book of Marvels* Phlegon does little editing, copying parts of whole documents into his work. Indeed, in mixing long lists of names with brief anecdotes and extensive quotations of prophetic poetry, the author seems not to have worked with a clear image of audience and purpose.

Ancient fascination with longevity found expression in ordinary wonder about the upper limit of human and other life, in speculation on the causes of longevity, in traditions about aston-ishingly long-lived individuals and nations and in other ways. Some of it is scientific in spirit, such as Aristotle's essay, 'On Length and Shortness of Life' (Περὶ μακροβιότητος καὶ βραχυβιότητος), in which he discusses physiological and envi-ronmental factors determining life-spans of different forms of life. But most of it is much less rigorous and two ancient treat-ments are similar enough to that of Phlegon to be mentioned here for the sake of comparison.

One is an extensive passage on longevity in Pliny's *Natural History* (7.153–64), composed in the century preceding Phlegon. Pliny begins by citing Hesiod, who he says was the first to make observations on the subject. According to the Greek poet, a crow lives for nine human lifetimes, a stag for four crow lifetimes, a raven for three stag lifetimes and the lifetimes of the phoenix and of nymphs are even longer (Hesiod fr. 304 MW). Pliny goes on to record anecdotal information from Greek poets and historians about the astonishing longevity of various persons and ethnic groups (for example, instances of people living hundreds of years), although he discounts some of these figures on the grounds that some peoples customarily count seasons as years. Moving on to what he regards as more reliable data he cites a number of men and women, mostly prominent Romans, who lived long lives. This leads into a discussion of views on the upper limit of human life and the astrological and environmental factors that may affect length of life. Admitting that the causes of longevity are uncertain, he turns finally to the most certain data of all, the records of the census held only a few years earlier (AD 74) by the Emperors Vespasian and Titus, and focusing upon a single region cites the name and town of several persons who attained a high age (e.g., Lucius Terentius, son of Marcus, at Bononia declared himself to be 135), and finishes with a few quick summaries (e.g., fifty-four persons declared themselves to be 100 years of age).

The other treatment is a Greek essay that has come down under the name of Lucian but was composed by an unknown author in the early third century AD. Pseudo-Lucian's *Long-Lived Persons* (Μακρόβιοι) is a learned anecdotal catalogue of the deaths of prominent men—no women are mentioned—who attained a long life. The author musters his material by the profession of his subjects rather than age attained: kings, philosophers, historians, orators, poets and others. The composition is a birthday gift to its addressee, to whom the composer wishes a long life, urging him to attend to his mind and body as did the persons described in the essay. But the injunction is only a friendly gesture, for the author makes no real attempt to isolate the factors that might have contributed to their longevity. See Wachsmuth 237–38; Franz Rühl, 'Die Makrobier des Lukianos', *RhM* 62, 1907, 421–37, and 'Noch Einmal die Makrobier des Lukianos', *RhM* 64, 1909, 137–50; and Christ 2: 738–39.

Pliny and Phlegon draw on mostly the same kinds of sources for their information: anecdotal biography and census data. Pliny's presentation is certainly the more sophisticated in that he orders his data into three levels of reliability rather than treating it as being of equal value, discusses possible factors accounting for unreliable data (different systems of counting) and for differences in human longevity (astrological and environmental variables) and summarizes the relevant census information rather than listing it in full. The difference is that Pliny writes as a scholar, Phlegon as a paradoxographer, and one little given to editing. Unlike the other two, Pseudo-Lucian's presentation is entirely anecdotal. His aim however is neither that of the scholarly encyclopaedist nor that of the collector of wonders but that of the rhetorician, to convey in a pleasant and convincing manner his wish that the recipient of the piece live long.

The *Olympiads* (Ὀλυμπιάδες) was circulated in several editions of different sizes. The full work contained sixteen books, a smaller edition had eight books and there was an epitome in two books. Only small pieces survive, which are sufficient to reveal its plan and format. It begins with a history of the founding of the Olympic Games, followed by chronological tables of Olympiads from the first Olympic Games (776 BC) until the 229th Olympiad (AD 137–40), when Hadrian died. For each Olympiad Phlegon gives the names of the Olympic victors and the competitions in which they were victorious as well as notable non-athletic events of the period—natural phenomena, omens, religious matters, births of notable persons, political activities, military successes and setbacks and the like. Whether he has invented this format or works in a tradition of such compilations is unknown. Inasmuch as less information was available for the earlier years, the treatment of the Olympiads generally becomes more detailed as they approach Phlegon's own times and for Hadrian's reign he had access to abundant materials. Some of the paradoxographical material that the compiler assembled for the chronicles possibly formed the basis of his *Book of Marvels*.

The Byzantine scholar Photios says he read the first five books of the *Olympiads*. Its Greek he describes as being neither too vulgar nor purely Attic in style, but he faults Phlegon's fondness for oracles, which he says the author quotes in excess, completely sating the reader, so that for Photios the work lacks all charm (*FGH* 257 T 3). Indeed, Phlegon's weakness for oracular verse is apparent in his *Book of Marvels* and *Long-Lived Persons*. I have already remarked upon his disinclination to edit, reflecting, it seems, an appreciation of interesting documents but an insensitivity to proportion. Nevertheless, to judge by the many ancient citations of the *Olympiads*, it was Phlegon's most successful work, and its author was occasionally praised. Eusebios calls him 'the distinguished calculator of Olympiads', and Hieron includes him in a list of 'very learned men' (*FGH* 257 F 16a and 24b). On the composition of the *Olympiads* see Wachsmuth 147–49; Weber 94–98; Jacoby *FGH*, Commentary 2: 838–45.

The principal usefulness of the *Olympiads* was as a chronology, for as units of time the Olympiads had for several centuries served Greek historians, although not ordinary persons in daily life, as a convenient system of absolute dating. An Olympiad was a period of four years, consisting of the year in which, sometime during the summer, the several-day Olympic festival fell, and of the three years that ensued before the next

Olympic festival. Several lists of Olympic victors had been compiled and published before Phlegon's, the first one by the sophist Hippias of Elis (fourth century BC), and various refinements of the idea—the numbering of successive Olympiads and the counting of years within Olympiads—had been introduced by Hippias's successors. Time within an Olympiad could be specified by reference to the ordinal year as, for example, the third year of the 149th Olympiad. See E.J. Bickerman, *Chronology of the Ancient World*, Ithaca 1968, especially 75–76. In his *Chronicle* Eusebios preserves a list for Olympiads 1–249, and fragments of earlier lists are printed in Jacoby (*FGH* 414–16).

In order to convey an idea of the work I translate the two largest fragments of *Olympiads*, one describing the founding of the Olympic Games, the other dealing with the victors and events of the 177th Olympiad.

The Texts

For the *Book of Marvels* and other works of Greek paradoxography I use Giannini's edition, noting any departures from it as they arise, and Jacoby's texts of *Olympiads* (*FGH* 257 F 1 and 12) and *Long-Lived Persons* (*FGH* 257 F 37). The numerals in the text are supplied by the editors, and the subtitles, except where otherwise indicated, by myself.

PART I

TEXTS

2

Book of Marvels

Ghosts

1 Philinnion

1 . . . [the nurse] went to the door of the guest room, and in the light of the burning lamp she saw the girl sitting beside
2 Machates. Because of the extraordinary nature of the sight, she did not wait there any longer but ran to the girl's mother screaming, 'Charito! Demostratos!' She said they should get up and come with her to their daughter, who was alive and by some divine will was with the guest in the guest room.
3 When Charito heard this astonishing report, the immensity of the message and the nurse's excitement made her frightened and faint. But after a short time the memory of her daughter came to her, and she began to weep; in the end she accused the old woman of being mad and told her to
4 leave her presence immediately. But the nurse replied boldly and reproachfully that she herself was rational and sound of mind, unlike her mistress, who was reluctant to see her own daughter.

With some hesitation Charito went to the door of the guest room, partly coerced by the nurse and partly wanting to know what really had happened. Since considerable time—about two hours—had now passed since the nurse's

original message, it was somewhat late when Charito went
5   to the door and the occupants were already asleep. She
peered in and thought she recognized her daughter's clothes
and features, but inasmuch as she could not determine the
truth of the matter she decided to do nothing further that
night. She planned to get up in the morning and confront the
girl, or if she should be too late for that she intended to question Machates thoroughly about everything. He would not,
she thought, lie if asked about so important a matter. And
so she said nothing and left.

6   At dawn, however, it turned out that by divine will or
chance the girl had left unnoticed. When Charito came to
the room she was upset with the young man because of the
girl's departure. She asked him to relate everything to her
from the beginning, telling the truth and concealing nothing.

7   The youth was anxious and confused at first, but hesi-
tantly revealed that the girl's name was Philinnion. He told
how her visits began, how great her desire for him was, and
that she said she came to him without her parents' knowledge. Wishing to make the matter credible he opened his
coffer and took out the items the girl had left behind—the
golden ring he had obtained from her and the breast-band
she had left the night before.

8   When Charito saw this evidence she uttered a cry, tore her
clothes, cast her headdress from her head and fell to the
ground, throwing herself upon the tokens and beginning her
9   grief anew. As the guest observed what was happening, how
all were grieving and wailing as if they were about to lay the
girl into her grave, he became upset and called upon them to
stop, promising to show them the girl if she came again.
Charito accepted this and bade him carefully keep his
promise to her.

10   Night came on and now it was the hour when Philinnion
was accustomed to come to him. The household kept watch,
wanting to know of her arrival. She entered at the usual time
and sat down on the bed. Machates pretended that nothing

was wrong, since he wished to investigate the whole incredible matter to find out if the girl he was consorting with, who took care to come to him at the same hour, was actually dead. As she ate and drank with him, he simply could not believe what the others had told him, and he supposed that some grave-robbers had dug into the tomb and sold the clothes and the gold to her father. But in his wish to learn exactly what the case was, he secretly sent his slaves to summon Demostratos and Charito.

11   They came quickly. When they first saw her they were speechless and panic-stricken by the amazing sight, but after that they cried aloud and embraced their daughter. Then Philinnion said to them: 'Mother and father, how unfairly you have grudged my being with the guest for three days in my father's house, since I have caused no one any pain. For this reason, on account of your meddling, you shall grieve all over again, and I shall return to the place appointed for me. For it was not without divine will that I came here.'

12   Immediately upon speaking these words she was dead, and her body lay stretched out visibly on the bed. Her father and mother threw themselves upon her, and there was much confusion and wailing in the house because of the calamity. The misfortune was unbearable and the sight incredible.

      The event was quickly heard through the city and was
13   reported to me. Accordingly, during the night I kept in check the crowds that gathered at the house, since, with news like this going from mouth to mouth, I wanted to make sure there would be no trouble.

14   By early dawn the theatre was full. After the particulars had been explained, it was decided that we should first go to the tomb, open it, and see whether the body lay on its bier or whether we would find the place empty. A half-year had
15   not yet passed since the death of the girl. When we opened the chamber into which all deceased members of the family were placed, we saw bodies lying on biers, or bones in the case of those who had died long ago, but on the bier onto

which Philinnion had been placed we found only the iron ring that belonged to the guest and the gilded wine cup, objects that she had obtained from Machates on the first day.

16   Astonished and frightened, we proceeded immediately to Demostratos's house to see if the corpse was truly to be seen in the guest room. After we saw the dead girl lying there on the ground, we gathered at the place of assembly, since the events were serious and incredible.

17   There was considerable confusion in the assembly and almost no one was able to form a judgment on the events. The first to stand up was Hyllos, who is considered to be not only the best seer among us but also a fine augur; in general, he has shown remarkable perception in his craft. He said we should burn the girl outside the boundaries of the city, since nothing would be gained by burying her in the ground within its boundaries, and perform an apotropaic sacrifice to Hermes Chthonios and the Eumenides. Then he prescribed that everyone purify himself completely, cleanse the temples and perform all the customary rites to the chthonic deities. He spoke to me also in private about the king and the events, telling me to sacrifice to Hermes, Zeus Xenios and Ares, and to perform these rites with care.

18   When he had made this known to us, we undertook to do what he had prescribed. Machates, the guest whom the ghost had visited, became despondent and killed himself.

If you decide to write about this to the king, send word to me also in order that I may dispatch to you one of the persons who examined the affair in detail.

Farewell.

2 Polykritos the Aitolarch

1   Hieron of Alexandria or of Ephesos relates that a ghost also appeared in Aitolia.

2   One of the citizens, a certain Polykritos, was voted

Aitolarch for a term of three years by the people, who
deemed him worthy among the citizens because of his and
his ancestors' nobility. While in office he took a Lokrian
woman as wife, lived with her for three nights, and departed
3   from life on the fourth night. The woman remained at home
as a widow. When the time for childbirth came she delivered
a child with two sets of genitals, male and female, which
differed amazingly in their nature. The upper portion of the
genitals was hard and manly, whereas the part around the
thighs was womanish and softer.

4   Struck with astonishment the child's relatives took it to the
agora where they called an assembly, summoned sacrificers
and diviners and deliberated about the child. Of these, some
declared that a breach would come about between the
Aitolians and the Lokrians, for the infant had been separated
from its mother, who was a Lokrian, and its father, an Aitolian.
Others thought that they should take the child and the mother
away to the countryside beyond the frontiers and burn them.

5   As they were deliberating, Polykritos, the man who had
previously died, appeared in the assembly near the child and
6   wearing black clothing. The citizens were stricken with
amazement at the apparition and many had begun to flee
when he called on them to take courage and not be thrown
into confusion at the presence of the ghost.

After he had put a stop to most of the commotion and
confusion, he spoke in a soft voice, as follows: 'Citizens, my
body is dead, but in the goodwill and kindness I feel towards
you I am alive. I am here with you now for your benefit,
having appealed to those who are master of things beneath
the earth. And so I call on you now, since you are fellow
citizens, not to be frightened or repulsed by the unexpected
presence of a ghost. I beg all of you, praying by the salvation of each one of you, to hand over to me the child I begot,
in order that no violence take place as a result of your
reaching some other decision and that your hostility towards
me not be the beginning of difficult and harsh troubles. For

it is not permitted me to let the child be burnt by you, just because of the madness of the seers who have made proclamations to you.

'Now, I excuse you because as you behold so strange a sight you are at a loss as to what is the right course of action for you to take. If, moreover, you will obey me without fear, you will be released from your present fear as well as the impending catastrophe. But if you come to some other opinion, I fear that because of your distrust of me you will fall into an irremedial calamity. Now because of the goodwill I had when I was alive, I have also now in this my present unexpected appearance foretold what is beneficial to you. So I ask you not to put me off any longer but to deliberate correctly and, obeying what I have said, to give me the child in an auspicious manner. For it is not permitted me to linger long on account of those who rule beneath the earth.'

7   After saying this he was quiet for a little while, expectantly awaiting whatever resolution they would bring forth concerning his request. Now, some thought they should hand over the child and make atonement for both the prodigy and the supernatural being that was standing by, but most disagreed, saying that they ought not to deliberate rashly, since the matter was of great importance and the problem was not an ordinary one.

8   Seeing that they were not heeding him but instead were hindering his desire, he spoke again: 'At all events, citizens, if trouble befalls you on account of your irresolution, blame not me but the fate that thus leads you down the wrong path, a fate that, opposing me also, forces me to act unlawfully against my own child.'

9   The people had clustered together and were arguing about the portent when the ghost took hold of the child, forced back most of the men, hastily tore the child limb

10   from limb, and began to devour him. People began to shout and throw stones at him in an attempt to drive him away. Unharmed by the stones, he consumed the entire body of the

boy except for his head, and then suddenly disappeared.

11   The people, vexed at these happenings and in a state of extraordinary perplexity, wanted to send a delegation to Delphi, but the head of the boy that was lying on the ground began to speak, foretelling the future in an oracle.

O countless folk inhabiting a land famed in song,
Do not go to the sanctuary of Phoibos, to the temple with
   its incense,
For the hands you hold in the air are unclean from blood,
The journey before your feet is defiled.
Renounce the journey to the tripod, and consider instead
   what I say,   5
For I will recount the entire behest of the oracle.
On this day in the course of a year
Death has been ordained for all, but by the will of Athena
The souls of Lokrians and Aitolians shall live mixed together.
Nor will there be a respite from evil, not even briefly,   10
For a bloody drizzle is poured on your heads,
Night keeps everything hidden, and a dark sky has spread
   over it,
At once night causes a darkness to move over the entire earth,
At home all the bereaved move their limbs at the threshold,
The woman will not leave off grieving, nor do the children 15
Leave off grieving for what they weep for in the halls, as
   they cling to their dear parents.
Such has been the wave that has crashed down upon
   everyone from above,
Alas, alas, without cease I bewail the terrible sufferings of
   my land
And my most dread mother, whom death eventually
   carried away.
All the gods will render inglorious the birth   20
Of whatever there remains of Aitolian and Locrian seed,
Because death has not touched my head, nor has it done
   away
With all the indistinguishable limbs of my body but has left
   [me on] the earth.
Come and expose my head to the rising dawn, and

Do not hide it below within the dusky earth.   25
As for you yourselves, abandon the land and
Go to another land, to a people of Athena,
If you choose an escape from death in accordance with fate.

12 When the Aitolians heard the oracle they brought their wives,
infant children and very elderly to such places of safety as
each man was able to arrange. They themselves remained
behind, awaiting what would occur and it happened in the
following year that the Aitolians and the Akarnanians joined
battle, with great destruction on both sides.

3 Bouplagos and Publius

1 Antisthenes the Peripatetic philosopher relates that the
consul Acilius Glabrio along with the legates Porcius
Cato and Lucius Valerius Flaccus drew up in battle-order
against Antiochos in Thermopylai and fought nobly,
forcing Antiochos's men to cast away their weapons and
Antiochos himself to flee with five hundred guards initially
to Elateia, after which Acilius compelled him to withdraw
to Ephesos.

2 Acilius dispatched Cato to Rome to report his victory while
he himself waged war against the Aitolians in Herakleia,
which he easily captured.

3   In the confrontation with Antiochos at Thermopylai, very
conspicuous omens occurred to the Romans. In the days
following Antiochos's failure and flight, the Romans occupied themselves in removing for burial the bodies of their
own fallen and in collecting arms and other spoils as well as
prisoners of war.

Bouplagos

4 There was a certain Bouplagos, a cavalry commander from
Syria who had been held in high esteem by King Antiochos
and had fallen after fighting nobly. At midday while the

Romans were gathering all the enemy's arms, Bouplagos stood up from among the dead, though he had twelve wounds, and went to the Roman camp where he proclaimed in a soft voice the following verses.

> Stop despoiling an army gone to the land of Hades,
> For already Zeus Kronides is angry beholding your ill
>   deeds,
> Wrothful at the slaughter of an army and at your
>   doings, and
> Will send a bold-hearted tribe against your land
> That will put an end to your rule, and you will pay for
>   what you have wrought.

5 Shaken by this utterance the generals quickly convened the multitude and deliberated about the ghost. They decided to cremate and bury Bouplagos (who had expired immediately after his utterance), purify the camp, perform a sacrifice to Zeus Apotropaios and send a delegation to Delphi to ask the god what they should do.

6 When the envoys reached Pytho and asked what to do, the Pythia proclaimed the following oracle.

> Restrain yourself now, Roman, and let justice abide
>   with you,
> Lest Pallas stir up a much greater Ares against you,
> And make desolate your market-places, and you, fool,
>   for all your effort,
> Lose much wealth before reaching your land.

7 When they had heard this oracle they renounced entirely the idea of waging war upon any of the peoples of Europe.

Breaking camp at the forementioned place they went to Naupaktos in Aitolia where there was a shared temple of the Greeks, and they prepared sacrifices at public expense and first fruits according to custom.

Publius

8   After the rites had been discharged, General Publius began
to rave and behave in a deranged manner, making many
utterances in a state of divine possession, of which some
were in verse and some in prose. When word of this matter
reached the ordinary soldiers, they all rushed to Publius's
tent, partly from anxiety and amazement that the best man
among them, an experienced leader, had fallen into such a
state and partly from a wish to hear what he was saying. As
a result some men were pressed together so powerfully that
they were suffocated.

The following utterance in verse was made by him while
he was still inside his tent.

> O my country, what a baneful Ares Athena will bring
>   you,
> When you ravage Asia with its great wealth and return
>   to
> Italian soil and the garlanded cities
> Of Thrinakia, lovely isle, which Zeus founded.   5
> For an army, brave and strong of spirit, will come
> From distant Asia whence are the risings of the sun,
> And a king crossing the narrow ford of the Hellespont
> Will make a faithful truce with an Epirote ruler.
> He will come to Ausonia after gathering an army
>   beyond counting
> From every part of Asia and lovely Europe, and   10
> Overpower you, making desolate your homes and
>   walled towns
> And enslaving you, taking away your day of freedom,
> On account of the wrath of great-hearted Athena.

9   After he had proclaimed these verses he darted out of his
tent in his tunic and made the following utterance in prose.

'I reveal, soldiers and citizens, that crossing over from
Europe to Asia you will overcome King Antiochos in battles
at sea and on land, and become master of all the land on this

side of the Tauros and of all the cities established in it,
having driven Antiochos into Syria; this land and these cities
will be handed over to the sons of Attalos. The Celts
dwelling in Asia who face you in battle will be worsted, and
you will take possession of their women and children and all
their household goods, and convey them to Europe. But
European coastal-dwellers, the Thracians of the Propontis
and Hellespont, will attack you around the land of the
Ainioi as you return from your campaign, killing some of
your men and capturing some of your booty. When the
others have come safely through and been conveyed to
Rome, there will be a treaty with King Antiochos, according
to which he will pay money and withdraw from a certain
region.'

10   When he had made this proclamation he cried out the
following in a loud voice.

'I see bronze-chested forces crossing over from Asia, kings
gathering together into one place, men of every nation
against Europe, and the din of horses, the clashing of spears,
gory slaughter, terrible plundering, the fall of towers, the
razing of city walls, and the unspeakable desolation of the
land.'

11   After this he spoke again in verse.

When the glimmering Nesaian horses with their
    frontlets of gold
Walk onto the illustrious land, leaving behind their
    pedestal
—those which once in the sumptuous city of the
    Syracusans
Eetion wrought in his artistry, strengthening lovely
    friendship:
He laid...   5
Golden, and on it he fitted the son of Hyperion
With rays and eyes gleaming—
At that time, Rome, your harsh sufferings will all be
    fulfilled.

For a broad host will come that will destroy your
    entire land,
Make desolate your market-places, waste your cities
    with fire,   10
Fill your rivers with blood, fill also Hades,
And bring upon you slavery, piteous, hateful, and
    obscure.
A wife will not welcome back her husband
Returned from war, but Hades clad in black beneath
    the earth
Will hold him among the deceased along with children
    robbed from their mothers,   15
And a foreign Ares will impose slavery's day.

12 After he had uttered this he fell silent, and proceeding
outside the camp he climbed up a certain oak tree. The
crowd followed, and he called to them: 'Romans and other
soldiers, it falls to me to die and be devoured by a huge red
wolf on this very day, but, as for you, know that everything
I have said is going to happen to you: take the imminent
appearance of the beast and my own destruction as proof
that I have spoken by divine intimation.'

Saying this, he told them to stand aside and not to prevent
the approach of the beast, saying that it would not be to
13 their benefit to drive it away. The crowd followed his
bidding, and presently the wolf came. When Publius saw it,
he came down from the oak tree and fell upon his back,
whereupon the wolf ripped him open and devoured him
while everyone looked on. Having consumed his body
14 except for his head it turned away to the mountain. When
the crowd now approached, wishing to take up the remains
and give them proper burial, the head, which lay on the
ground, proclaimed these verses:

Touch not my head. For it is not right
For those in whose hearts Athena has placed wild
    anger

To take hold of a sacred head. But stop
And listen to the prophecy by means of which I shall
   declare the truth to you.
To this land there will come a great and powerful Ares, 5
Who will dispatch the armed folk to Hades in the
   darkness below and
Shatter the stone towers and the long walls.
Siezing our wealth, our infant children, and our wives
He will bring them to Asia, crossing over the waves.
These sure truths Phoibos Apollo has spoken to you,   10
The Pythian, who sent his powerful servant and
Led me to the abode of the blessed and of Persephone.

15   When they heard this they were extremely upset. After constructing a temple to Apollo Lykios and an altar at the place where the head lay, they embarked on their ships, and each person sailed to his own land. Everything foretold by Publius came to pass.

Sex-Changers and Hermaphrodites

4 Teiresias

1   Hesiod, Dikaiarchos, Klearchos, Kallimachos and certain other authors relate the following incident about Teiresias. They say that Teiresias, son of Eueres, saw some snakes copulating on the mountain in Kyllene in Arkadia, wounded the other of them, and forthwith changed form. He went from being a man to being a woman, and had intercourse
2   with a man. Apollo informed him in an oracle that if he observed the creatures copulating and similarly wounded the one snake, he would be as he was before. Watching for an opportunity Teiresias did what the god had said and thereby recovered his former nature.
3   Zeus and Hera had a quarrel, he claiming that in sexual intercourse the woman had a larger share of pleasure than

the man did, and she claiming the opposite. They decided to send for Teiresias and ask him, inasmuch as he had experienced both. When they enquired of him he declared that a man enjoyed one-tenth of the pleasure and a woman nine-

4   tenths. Hera angrily gouged out his eyes, making him blind, but Zeus gave him the gift of prophecy and a life-span of seven generations.

5 Kainis

1   The same authors relate that in the land of the Lapiths a daughter was born to King Elatos and named Kainis.

2   After Poseidon had had sexual intercourse with her and promised to fulfill any wish for her, she asked that he change

3   her into a man and render her invulnerable. Poseidon granted her request, and her name was changed to Kaineus.

6 An Unnamed Maiden

1   There was also a hermaphrodite in Antioch by the Maeander River when Antipater was archon at Athens and Marcus Vinicius and Titus Statilius Taurus, surnamed Corvinus, were consuls in Rome.

2   A maiden of prominent family, thirteen years of age, was good-looking and had many suitors. She was betrothed to the man whom her parents wished, the day of the wedding was at hand, and she was about to go forth from her house when suddenly she experienced an excruciating pain and

3   cried out. Her relations took charge of her, treating her for stomach pains and colic, but her suffering continued for three days without a break, perplexing everyone about the nature of her illness. Her pains let up neither during the night nor during the day, and although the doctors in the city tried every kind of treatment they were unable to discover the cause of her illness. At around daybreak of the fourth day her pains became stronger, and she cried out with

a great wailing. Suddenly male genitals burst forth from her, and the girl became a man.

4   Some time later she was brought to the Emperor Claudius in Rome. Because of the portent he had an altar built on the Capitoline to Jupiter the Averter of Evil.

7 Philotis

1   There was also a hermaphrodite in Mevania, a town in Italy, in the country house of Agrippina Augusta when Dionysodoros was archon in Athens, and Decimus Iunius Silanus Torquatus and Quintus Haterius Antoninus were consuls in Rome.

2   A maiden named Philotis, whose family came from Smyrna, was of marriageable age and had been betrothed to a man by her parents when male genitals appeared in her and she became a man.

8 Sympherousa

There was another hermaphrodite at this same time in Epidauros, a child of poor family, who earlier was called Sympherousa but upon becoming a man was named Sympheron. He spent his life as a gardener.

9 Aitete

Likewise in Syrian Laodikeia there was a woman named Aitete, who underwent a change in form and name even while she was living with her husband. Having become a man Aitete was renamed Aitetos. This happened when Makrinos was archon at Athens, and Lucius Lamia Aelianus and Sextus Carminius Veterus were consuls in Rome.

I myself have seen this person.

10 Sibylline Oracles

1   A hermaphrodite was also begotten in Rome when Jason
was archon in Athens and Marcus Plautius Hypsaeus and
Marcus Fulvius Flaccus were consuls in Rome.

     Because of the event the Senate decreed that the priests
should read the Sibylline oracles, and they made atonement
2   and narrated the oracles. The oracles are as follows.

First Oracle

The fate of mortals, who only afterwards learn what place
    each person is to go,   1a
And all the prodigies and plagues of the goddess Destiny   1
This loom of mine will reveal, if you consider these things
    in your mind,
Trusting in its strength. I declare that one day a woman will
    bear
A hermaphrodite having all the male parts
And all the parts that infant female women manifest.   5
I shall no longer conceal but declare to you
    straightforwardly
Sacrifices for Demeter and holy Persephone,
By means of my loom, sovereign goddess that I am,
    [sacrifices that you should perform], if you obey me,
For very august Demeter and holy Persephone.
First gather together a treasure of coin,   10
Whatever you wish, from the cities with their mingled tribes
    and from yourselves,
And arrange a sacrifice to be offered to Kore's mother,
    Demeter.
Thrice nine bulls at public expense I bid you
... (seven lines missing)   13a–g
To sacrifice bright, fine-horned, white-haired, if
They seem to you to be of surpassing beauty.   15
Bid the same number of girls as I mentioned earlier perform
    this rite in the Greek manner,
Praying to the deathless queen with offerings

Solemnly and purely. Thereafter let her receive
Lasting sacrifices from your wives, and during your lifetime,
    Trusting in my loom, let persons carry bright light   20
To most holy Demeter. Second, let them take
Thrice as many offerings [as earlier], unmixed with wine,
    and place them into the ravening fire—
This should be done by the old women who are knowledge-
    able about offerings.
Let all other females zealously make the same number of
    offerings for Ploutonis,
Girls who have minds fresh-budding in their age,   25
Children, let them all pray to holy, learned Ploutonis
To remain in the land if war prevails,
And for forgetfulness of war and city to enter their hearts.
Let youths and maidens bear treasure there
… (three lines missing)

Second Oracle

… (many lines missing)
In my divinely-fashioned loom, and with multicoloured
    weavings   30
Let holy Ploutonis be adorned, that there be a check against
    evils.
That which is most beautiful and wished for on earth
For mortals to see, let it be carried zealously
To the royal maiden as a gift mixed with the loom.
And when [you pray] to Demeter and pure Persephone   35
To ward off the yoke from your land forever,
[Offer] to Aidoneus Plouton the blood of a dark-haired ox
Attired in splendid garments, with the help of a herdsman,
    who
Trusting in the oracle's purpose will slaughter the ox
In the company of all other men in the land who trust
    [in its purpose].   40
Let no disbeliever be present at the sacrifices,
But let him rather stand apart where it is customary for
    disbelievers to be,

And perform a sacrifice that is not eaten.
But whoever comes to it knowing our oracle,
Let him seek out holy lord Phoibos in sacrifices,   45
Zealously burning rich thigh-bones on his altars,
[Sacrificing] the youngest of the bright goats. And, you know,
Let the supplicant garland his head and beseech Phoibos Paieon
For a release from the evil that is impending,
And when he returns from this, [let him beseech] royal
     mistress Hera,   50
Sacrificing a white cow according to ancestral custom in the
     land.
To sing a hymn, those females belonging to the foremost
     families among the people,
... (two verses missing)   52a–b
When the inhabitants of the islands
Earnestly settle in the Cumaean land of their opponents by
     force, not deceit,
Let them establish an image of holy Queen Hera   55
And a temple in the ancestral manner.
[The evil] will come—if you [do] all this and trust in my words,
Going to the most holy queen with sacrifices and   (58)
Performing the wineless rites for as many days as there are
     in the year,   (60)
Long and into the future—but not in your time.   (59)
The man who does so will have power forever.
Prepare wineless offerings and sheep, and sacrifice them to
     the chthonic gods.
When you have great temples of Hera everywhere
And when there are hewn images and the other things I
     have said, know well,
On my leaves—at the behest of my shuttle   65
I covered my lovely eyes with my veil when I picked up the
     glorious leaves
Of the fruitful grey olive-tree—[you will find] a release from
     evils. When
The time comes for you in which you have other newborn
     creatures,
Then a Trojan will liberate you from your miseries and
     from the land of Greece.

But since I have moved to another subject, in what 70
    direction do you urge my speaking to go?
...(end missing)

Finds of Giant Bones

11 Idas

1   In Messene not many years ago, as Apollonios says, it
happened that a storage jar made of stone broke apart in a
powerful storm when it was pounded by much water, and
there came out of it the triple head of a human body. It had

2   two sets of teeth. They sought to discover whose head it
was, and the inscription explained it: 'Idas' was inscribed
thereon. So the Messenians prepared another storage jar at
public expense, placed the hero in it, and tended him more
carefully, since they perceived that he was the man about
whom Homer says

> And of Idas, who of men on earth at that time
> Was the strongest. He drew his bow against lord Phoibos
> Apollo for the sake of his lovely-ankled bride.

12 The Cave of Artemis

In Dalmatia in the so-called Cave of Artemis one can see
many bodies whose rib-bones exceed eleven cubits.

13–14 A Giant Tooth

(13) Apollonios the grammarian reports that in the time of
Tiberius Nero there was an earthquake in which many
notable cities of Asia Minor utterly disappeared, which
Tiberius subsequently rebuilt at his own expense. On
account of this the people constructed and dedicated to him
a colossus beside the temple of Aphrodite, which is in the

Roman forum, and also set up statues in a row next to it from each of the cities.

1   (14) Among the places that suffered from the earthquake were numerous cities in Sicily as well as the regions around Rhegium, and numerous peoples in Pontus were also struck.

2   In the cracks in the earth huge bodies appeared that the local inhabitants were hesitant to move, although as a sample they sent to Rome a tooth of one of the bodies. It was not

3   just a foot long but even greater than this measurement. The delegates showed it to Tiberius and asked him if he wished the hero to be brought to him. Tiberius devised a shrewd plan such that, while not depriving himself of a knowledge of its size, he avoided the sacrilege of the robbing of the

4   dead. He summoned a certain geometer, Pulcher by name, a man of some renown whom he respected for the man's skill, and bade him fashion a face in proportion to the size of the tooth. The geometer estimated how large the entire body as well as the face would be by means of the weight of the tooth, hastily made a construction, and brought it to the emperor. Tiberius, saying that the sight of this was sufficient for him, sent the tooth back to where it had come from.

15 An Exhibit of Bones

1   One should not disbelieve the foregoing narrative, since in Nitriai in Egypt bodies are exhibited that are no smaller than these and are not concealed in the earth but are unencumbered and plain to see. The bones do not lie mixed together in disorder but are arranged in such a manner that a person viewing them recognizes some as thigh bones others as shin bones and so on with the other limbs.

2   One should not disbelieve in these bones either, considering that in the beginning when nature was in her prime she reared everything near to gods, but just as time is running down, so also the sizes of creatures have been shrinking.

16 Rhodes

I have also heard reports of bones in Rhodes that are so huge that in comparison the human beings of the present day are greatly inferior in size.

17 The Coffin of Makroseiris

The same author says that there was a certain island near Athens that the Athenians wanted to fortify. As they were digging foundations for the walls they found a coffin that was a hundred cubits long and in which there lay a withered body matching the coffin in size. On the coffin was the following inscription:

I, Makroseiris, am buried on a small isle
After living a life of five thousand years.

18 Carthage

Eumachos says in his *Geographical Description* that when the Carthaginians were surrounding their territory with a trench they found in the course of their digging two withered bodies lying in coffins. One of them was twenty-four cubits in structure, the other twenty-three.

19 Bosporos

1 Theopompos of Sinope says in his work *On Earthquakes* that in the Cimmerian Bosporos there was a sudden earthquake, as a result of which one of several ridges in that region was torn open, discharging huge bones. The skeletal

2 structure was found to be of twenty-four cubits. He says the local barbarian inhabitants cast the bones into the Maiotis Sea.

Monstrous Births

20 Multiple Features

A child was brought to Nero that had four heads and a proportionate number of limbs when the archon at Athens was Thrasyllos, and the consuls in Rome were Publius Petronius Turpilianus and Caesennius Paetus.

21 Multiple Features

Another child was born with a head growing out of its left shoulder.

22 Animal Child

An extraordinary omen occurred in Rome when the archon at Athens was Deinophilos and the consuls in Rome were Quintus Veranius and Gaius Pompeius Gallus. A highly respected maidservant belonging to the wife of Raecius Taurus, a man of praetorian rank, brought forth a monkey.

23 Partly-Animal Child

The wife of Cornelius Gallicanus gave birth near Rome to a child having the head of Anubis, when the archon at Athens was Demostratos and the consuls in Rome were Aulus Licinius Nerva Silianus and Marcus Vestinus Atticus.

24 Animal Children

A woman from the town of Tridentum in Italy brought forth snakes that were curled up into a ball, when the consuls in Rome were Domitian Caesar for the ninth time and Petilius Rufus for the second time and there was no archon in Athens.

25 Multiple Features

In Rome a certain woman brought forth a two-headed baby, which on the advice of the sacrificing priests was cast into the River Tiber. This happened when the archon at Athens was Hadrian, who later was emperor, and the consuls at Rome were the Emperor Trajan for the sixth time and Titus Sextius Africanus.

Births from Males

26 A Homosexual

The doctor Dorotheos says in his *Reminiscences* that in Egyptian Alexandria a male homosexual gave birth, and that because of the marvel the newborn infant was embalmed and is still preserved.

27 A Slave

The same thing occurred in Germany in the Roman army, which was under the command of Titus Curtilius Mancias: a male slave of a soldier gave birth. This happened while Konon was archon in Athens and Quintus Volusius Saturninus and Publius Cornelius Scipio were consuls in Rome.

Amazing Multiple Births

28 An Alexandrian Woman

Antigonos reports that in Alexandria a certain woman gave birth to twenty children in the course of four deliveries and that most of them were reared.

29 Another Alexandrian Woman

1   Another woman from the same city brought forth five children at one time, three of whom were male and two female,
whom the Emperor Trajan ordered to be reared at his own
2   expense. In the following year the same woman gave birth
to another three.

30 Aigyptos

Hippostratos says in his book *On Minos* that Aigyptos
begot fifty sons with one wife Euryrrhoe, daughter of
Neilos.

31 Danaos

Likewise Danaos had fifty daughters with a single wife,
Europe, daughter of Neilos.

Abnormally Rapid Development

32 An Unnamed Male

Krateros, the brother of King Antigonos, says he is aware
of a person who in the space of seven years was a child, a
youth, a man and an old man, and then died, having married
and begotten children.

33 Women in Pandaia

Megasthenes says that the women who dwell in Pandaia give
birth when they are six years old.

Discoveries of Live Centaurs

34–35 Hippocentaurs

1   (34) A hippocentaur was found in Saune, a city in Arabia, on a very high mountain that teems with a deadly drug. The drug bears the same name as the city and among fatal substances it is extremely quick and effective.

2   The hippocentaur was captured alive by the king, who sent it to Egypt together with other gifts for the emperor. Its sustenance was meat. But it did not tolerate the change of air, and died, so that the prefect of Egypt embalmed it and sent it to Rome.

3   At first it was exhibited in the palace. Its face was fiercer than a human face, its arms and fingers were hairy and its ribs were connected with its front legs and its stomach. It had the firm hooves of a horse and its mane was tawny, although as a result of the embalming its mane along with its skin was becoming dark. In size it did not match the usual representations, though it was not small either.

(35) There were also said to have been other hippocentaurs in the city of Saune mentioned above.

So far as concerns the one sent to Rome, anyone who is sceptical can examine it for himself, since as I said above it has been embalmed and is kept in the emperor's storehouse.

3

Long-Lived Persons

I Persons Who Have Lived a Hundred Years

Italians who have lived a hundred years, as I have ascertained not cursorily but from the census figures themselves.

1 Lucius Cornelius, son of Lucius, of the town of Placentia.
2 Lucius Glaucius Verus, son of Lucius, of the town of Placentia.
3 Lucius Vetustius Secundus, son of Lucius, of the town of Placentia.
4 Lucius Licinius Palus, freedman of Lucius, of the town of Placentia.
5 Lucius Acilius Marcellus, son of Lucius, of the town of Placentia.
6 Lucius Vettius, son of Marcus, [of the town] of Brixellum.
7 Lucius Cusonius, son of Lucius, of the town of Cornelia.
8 Lucius Gabinius, son of Lucius, of the town of Veleia.
9 Gaius Hortensius Fronto, son of Sextus, of the town of Bononia.
10 Gaius Nonius Maximus, son of Publius, of the town of Brixellum.
11 Gaius Amurius Tiro, son of Gaius, of the town of Cornelia.
12 Gaius Cassius Pudes, son of Titus, of the town of Parma.
13 Gaius Titius Communis, freedman of Gaius, of the town of Parma.

14 Gaius Vatius Tertius, son of Spurius, of the town of Placentia.
15 Gaius Iulius Pothus, . . . , of the town of Ravenna.
16 Gaius Valerius Primus, son of Quintus, of the town of Veleia.
17 Caesellius Cyrus, . . . , of the town of Placentia.
18 Catia, daughter of Gaius, of the town of Faventia.
19 Publius Fulvius Phryx, freedman of Lucius, of the town of Pollesia.
20 Publius Naevius, son of Lucius, of the town of Basileia.
21 Publius Decennius Demosthenes, freedman of Publius, of the town of Ariminum.
22 Petronia, [daughter] of Quintus, freedwoman of Lucius, of the town of Placentia.
23 Pollia Polla, daughter of Spurius, of the town of Aetosia.
24 Marcus Vilonius Severus, of the town of Veleia.
25 Marcus Terentius Albius, freedman of Marcus, of the town of Placentia.
26 Marcus Antonius, son of Lucius, of the town of Placentia.
27 Marcus Talpius Vitalis, son of Marcus, of the town of Placentia.
28 Marcus Acilius, son of Marcus, of the town of Bononia.
29 Marcus Nirellius, son of Gaius, of the town of Parma.
30 Titus Vibius Thalbius, son of Spurius, of the town of Parma.
31 Titus Aemilius, son of Quintus, of the town of Regium.
32 Titus Veteranius, son of Publius, of the town of Bononia.
33 Titus Numerius, son of Titus, of the town of Placentia.
34 Titus Servius Secundus, son of Titus, of the town of Bononia.
35 Titus Petronius, son of Spurius, of the town of Placentia.
36 Titus Antonius, son of Marcus, of the town of Regium.
37 Titus Aerusius Pollio, son of Gaius, of the town of Bononia.
38 Titus Camurius Tertius, son of Titus, of the town of Fidentia.
39 Turellia Forensis, freedwoman of Gaius, of the town of Bononia.
40 Quintus Cassius Rufus, son of Quintus, of the town of Regium.
41 Quintus Lucretius Primus, son of Quintus, of the town of Regium.

42 Quintus Velius, son of Publius, of the town of Veleia.
43 Antonia Secunda, daughter of Publius, of the town of Veleia.
44 Albatia Sabina, . . . , of the town of Parma.
45 Salvia Varena, daughter of Publius, of the town of Basileia.
46 Bebia Marcella, daughter of Sextus, of the town of Ortisia.
47 Bascia, [daughter] of Astikosos, Macedonian from Philippi.
48 Bonzes, [son] of Tonos, of Paroikopolis, Macedonian.
49 Phronton, [son] of Alboutios, Macedonian from Philippi.
50 Sarke, [daughter] of Skilas, Macedonian woman, Amphipolitan.
51 Aidesios, [son] of Dizas, of Paroikopolis, Macedonian.
52 Bithys, [son] of Dizastos, of Paroikopolis in Macedonia.
53 Zaikedenthes, [son] of Moukasos, Paroikopolitan, Macedonian.
54 Mantis, [son] of Kaiprizos, Macedonian, from Amphipolis.
55 Alexander, [son] of Demetrios, Tianian from Pontos and Bithynia.
56 Gaza, [daughter] of Timon, Tianian from Pontos and Bithynia.
57 Chreste, [daughter] of Antipatros, Tianian.
58 Chrysion, [daughter] of Theophilos, Tianian.
59 Hieron, [son] of Hieron, Tianian.
60 Mouzakos, [son] of Moukantios, of Nikomedeia in Bithynia.
61 Lucius Fidiclanius Nepos, Sinopian.
62 Aloukios Apilioutas, from the town of Interamnesia, Lusitania.
63 Ambatos, son of Dokourios, of the same town.
64 Kamalos, son of Kantolgounios, of the same town.
65 Keltios, son of Pellios, of the town of Apeilokarios.
66 Arruntius, son of Appius, of the town of Conimbrigesia.
67 Tamphios, son of Keltios, of the same town.
68 Dokkourios, son of Aloukkios, of the town of Aibourobisyngesia.

II Persons who were registered as being from one hundred and one to one hundred and ten years

69 Gaius Leledius Primus, . . . , of the town of Bononia: one hundred and one years.

70 Clodia Potestas, freedwoman of Gaius, of the town of Bononia: 101 years.

71 Cusinia Moschis, freedwoman of Gaius, of the town of Cornelia: 101 years.

72 Cereonia Verecunda, freedwoman of Publius, of the town of Cornelia: 101 years.

73 Livia Attica, freedwoman of Publius, of the town of Parma: 101 years.

74 Buria Lychnainis, . . . , of the town of Parma: 101 years.

75 Gaius Samius, son of Gaius, of the town of Veleia: 102 years.

76 Quintus Cornelius, son of Quintus, of the town of Regium: 102 years.

77 Titus Antonius, son of Titus, of the town of Parma: 102 years.

78 Cocnania Musa, . . . , of the town of Cornelia: 103 years.

79 Demokritos of Abdera: 104 years. He died after abstaining from food.

80 Ktesibios the historian: 104 years. He died while walking, as Apollodoros explains in his *Chronicles*.

81 Hieronymos the author of prose works. After spending considerable time in military campaigns, he collapsed and died from the many wounds he had received in wars. He lived 104 years, as Agatharchides says in the ninth book of his *Researches on Asia*.

82 Gaius Lallias Tionaeus, son of Lucius, of the town of Bononia: 105 years.

83 Publius Quisentius Ephyrion, freedman of Publius, of the town of Bononia: 105 years.

84 Titus Cottinas Chrysanthos, freedman of Titus, of the town of Faventia: 105 years.

85 Marcus Pomponius Severus, son of Marcus, of the town of Tannetana: 105 years.
86 Sextus Naevius, son of Sextus, of the town of Parma: 105 years.
87 Lucius Aelius Dorotheos, freedman of Lucius, of the town of Bononia: 106 years.
88 Gaius Pompusius Montianus, son of Publius: 107 years.
89 Polla Donata, daughter of Sextus, of the town of Bononia: 110 years.
90 Munantia Procula, daughter of Lucius, of the town of Regium: 110 years.

III Persons registered as being from 110 to 120 years

91 Titus Purennius Tutus, son of Lucius, of the town of Cornelia: 111 years.
92 Lucius Antistius Soterichos, freedman of Lucius, of the town of Ravenna: 113 years.
93 Lucius, [son] of Petrus, of the town of Cornelia: 114 years.
94 Iulia Modestina, of the town of Corsioli, ...
95 . . . , freedwoman of the centurion . . . , a woman still alive in our day, of the town of Brixellum: 120 years.
... (section probably missing)

IV Persons registered as being from 130 to 140 years

96 Lucius Terentius, son of Marcus, of the town of Bononia: 135 years.
97 Faustus, a slave of the emperor, from Sabini, at the Palatine Praetorium: 136 years. I saw this man myself when he was displayed to the Emperor Hadrian.

V ...

98 Arganthonios the king of the Tartesians, as Herodotos and
Anakreon the poet report: 150 years.

2 ...

99 The Sibyl of Erythrai lived just short of a thousand years, as
she herself says in her oracle in the following way.

But why, lamentable for the sufferings of others,
 Do I prophesy oracles, holding onto my own mad fate
 And experiencing my own painful gadfly?
 Now in the tenth life-span I possess a grievous old age,
 Raving among mortals, speaking the incredible,   5
 Foreseeing in visions all the trying cares of humankind.
 At that time glorious Leto's son, resenting
 My power of divination, his destructive heart filled with
      passion,
 Will release the soul imprisoned in my mournful
 Body, shooting my frame with a flesh-smiting arrow,   10
 Whereupon my soul, fluttering into the air
 And commingling with the wind, will send to mortals' ears
 Omens woven together with shrewd riddling.
 But my body will lie shamefully unburied on
 Mother earth, for no mortal will heap up a mound for me 15
 Or conceal me with a tomb. My dark blood
 Will sink down into the wide-wayed earth, in the withering
      of time.
 Thence it will produce shoots of abundant grass
 That will enter the livers of grazing sheep and
 Reveal the will of the gods by means of divination,   20
 And when the feather-clad birds feed on my flesh,
 They will occupy themselves with true prophecy for
      mortals.

3   In this oracle she shows that she has lived among humans
     for ten life spans and that after her departure from life her
     soul will be carried through the air, join the utterances that
     people make, and produce the omens that arise in speech;
     and the flesh of her unburied body will be eaten by the birds,
     who will signal prophecies by means of their behaviour,
     whereas the rest of her will moulder into the earth, and the
     flocks of sheep, eating of the grass that springs up from the
     earth, will bring the art of liver divination into human life.

4   The Sibyl represents a life span as being one hundred and
     ten years in her oracle for the Romans that deals with the
     Secular Games, which the Romans call *Saecularia*. When the
     allies and partners of the Romans were not abiding by their
     treaties but frequently were changing sides and making war
     on the Romans, the Sibyl prophesied that once the present
     Games were finished the Latins who had revolted would be
     subdued. The oracle is as follows.

When the longest span of life for humans passes,
Having journeyed its cycle of a hundred and ten years,
Remember, Roman, even if it escapes your notice,
Remember all these things: to sacrifice
To the immortal gods on the field along the boundless
      waters of the Tiber   5
At its narrowest point, when night comes upon earth
And the sun has hidden its own light. Perform a sacrifice
Of dark sheep and goats to the all-generating Moirai
And also appease childbirth-promoting Eileithyia
With offerings in the proper way. In that place   10
Let a black sow swollen with piglets be sacrificed to Gaia,
And let all-white bulls be led to the altar of Zeus
By day, not by night, for to the Ouranian gods
Sacrifices are performed in daylight. So must you yourself
Sacrifice. Let Hera's shining temple   15
Receive a young steer from you, and let Phoibos Apollo,
Who is also called Helios, receive equal victims,
Leto's son. Let Latin paeans
Sung by youths and maidens occupy the temple

Of the immortals. Let the maidens have a dancing place
   apart,   20
And let the boys, male progeny, likewise be apart, but
All must have living parents, the stock flourishing on both
   sides.
Let women tamed by the yoke of marriage sit bent-kneed
Alongside Hera's celebrated altar that day
And beseech the goddess. Give lustral agents   25
To all the men and women, especially to the females.
Let everyone carry from his house all that it is proper
For mortals to convey, who are offering first fruits of their
   sustenance,
Propitiations for the gracious spirits and blessed
Ouranian gods, and let all these things lie in store   30
Until the offerings... sacrificial hearths...
... for women and men as they sit...
Whence remember to make them ready. During the
   following days
And nights let there be a teeming gathering
At seats fit for gods, and let solemnity mix with laughter. 35
Remember to keep these injunctions always in mind, and
All Italian earth and all the earth of the Latins
Will always bear the yoke on its neck under your rule.

Phlegon of Tralleis, freedman of the emperor: Book of Wonders
and Long-Lived Persons.

4

Olympiads

Fragment 1

Founding of the Olympic Games

1   Phlegon, freedman of the Emperor Hadrian: On the Olympic Games.

    I think I should explain how the Olympic Games came to be founded, which is as follows. After Peisos, Pelops and Herakles, the first persons to have established the festival and the contest at Olympia, the Peloponnesians left off the religious observance for a while, namely, for a period of twenty-seven Olympiads, reckoning from Iphitos to Koroibos the Elean; and after they neglected the contest there was an uprising in the Peloponnese.

2   Lykourgos the Lakedaimonian, son of Prytanis, son of Eurypon, son of Soos, son of Proklees, son of Aristodemos, son of Aristomachos, son of Kleodaios, son of Hyllos, son of Herakles and Deianeira; and Iphitos, son of Haimon (or, as some say, of Praxonides, one of the descendents of Herakles), an Elean; and Kleosthenes, son of Kleonikos, of Pisa, wanting to re-establish concord and peace in the population, decided to restore the Olympic festival to its former customs and to hold a contest for unclothed competitors.

3   Men were sent to Delphi to inquire of the god whether he

approved of their carrying out these projects, and the god,
saying that it would be better to do so, ordered them to
announce an armistice to the cities that wanted to parti-
4   cipate in the contest. After the message had been carried
around, the disc was inscribed for the Hellanodikai, in
accordance with which they were to conduct the Olympic
5   Games. When the Peloponnesians, disliking the contest, did
not give their approval to it at all, a plague came upon them
and they suffered harm from a loss of their crops. So they
sent Lykourgos and his men back to ask for a cessation of
6   the plague and for healing. The Pythia gave the following
oracle:

> O dwellers in the Pelopian acropolis famed of the
>   whole earth,   1
> Ambassadors and most excellent of all men,
> Consider the god's oracle that I utter.
> Zeus is wrathful towards you because of the rites he
>   revealed by oracle,
> Because you are dishonouring the Olympic Games of
>   Zeus, universal ruler—   5
> Peisos was the first to found and institute his worship,
>   and
> After him Pelops, when he came to Greek land,
> Establishing a festival and contests in honour of the
>   dead
> Oinomaos, and third, in addition to these two, the
>   child of Amphitryon,
> Herakles, brought about a festival and contest for his
>   perished maternal uncle,   10
> Tantalid Pelops, the contest and rite that you, it seems,
> Are abandoning. Angry at this in his heart
> He has caused a terrible famine among you and a
>   plague, which
> You can end by re-establishing his festival.

7   When they had heard this they reported it to the
Peloponnesians. But the Peloponnesians did not trust the

oracle and by general decree sent them back again to enquire more exactly of the god concerning his response. The Pythia spoke as follows.

> O dwellers in the Peloponnese, go and sacrifice
> Around an altar, and obey whatever the seers say.

8   After they had received this oracle the Peloponnesians allowed the Eleans to institute the contest of the Olympic festival and to announce a truce to the cities.

9   Subsequently the Eleans, wanting to give aid to the Lakedaimonians when they were besieging Helos, sent a delegation to Delphi to consult the oracle. The Pythia gave this oracle:

> Ministers of the Eleans, guides of the laws of your
>   forebears,
> Guard your own homeland, abstain from war, and
> Lead the Greeks in a friendship of common right
> Whenever the kindly fourth year comes.

After they had received this oracle they abstained from war and took charge of the Olympic Games.

Crowns for the Victors

10   No one was crowned for the first five Olympiads, but in the sixth they decided to ask the oracle if they should bestow chaplets upon the victors. They sent King Iphitos to the shrine of the god, and the god said the following.

> Iphitos, place not the produce of sheep on victory,
> But bestow the wild and fruitful olive-tree
> That is now enveloped by the fine webs of a spider.

11 So he went to Olympia where there were many wild olive-
trees in the sanctuary, and finding one that was enveloped by
spider webs, he built a wall around it. Garlands were given
to the winners from this tree.

The first person to be crowned was Daikles of Messene,
who won the stadium race in the eighth Olympiad.

Fragment 12

Victors in the 177th Olympic Games

1 Hekatomnos the Milesian won three times: stadium race,
double course and hoplite race.

2 Hypsikles of Sikyon: long course.

Gaius of Rome: long course.

Aristonymidas of Kos: pentathlon.

Isodoros of Alexandria: wrestling, not thrown in the Circuit.

Atyanas, son of Hippokrates, of Adramyttion: boxing.

Sphodrias of Sikyon: pankration.

Sosigenes of Asia: boys' stadium race.

Apollophanes of Kyparissai: boys' wrestling.

Soterichos of Elis: boys' boxing.

Kalas of Elis: boys' pankration.

Hekatomnos of Miletos: hoplite race. He was crowned
three times in the same Olympiad—stadium race, double
course and hoplite race.

The four-horse chariot owned by Aristolochos of Elis.

The riding horse owned by Hegemon of Elis.

The pair of horses owned by Hellanikos of Elis.

The four-colt chariot owned by the same man.

The pair of colts owned by Kletias of Elis.

The riding colt owned by Kallippos of Elis.

Notable Events during the Olympiad.

3   Lucullus was besieging Amisos. Leaving Murena at the siege
with two divisions, he himself went ahead with three others
to Cabira, where he spent the winter. He ordered Hadrianus
to make war on Mithridates. He did so and overcame him.

4   There was an earthquake in Rome and many buildings
5   collapsed. And many other things happened in this
Olympiad.

6   In the third year of the Olympiad, 910,000 Romans were
7   enrolled at the census. Phraates, nicknamed 'God',
8   succeeded King Sinatroukas of Parthia upon his death.
9   Patron succeeded Phaidros the Epicurean. The poet Vergilius
Maro was born in this year on the Ides of October.

10   In the fourth year Tigranes and Mithridates collected
40,000 infantry and 30,000 cavalry and, deploying them in
the Italian manner, made war on Lucullus. Lucullus was
victorious. Five thousand men with Tigranes fell, and a
larger number was taken captive, apart from the rest of

11   the rabble. Catulus consecrated the Capitol in Rome.
12   Metellus set out for the Cretic war with three divisions,
came to the island, and after being victorious over Lasthenes

13   was proclaimed Imperator. He besieged the Cretans. The
pirate Athenodoros utterly reduced the Delians to slavery
and mutilated the statues of the so-called gods. Gaius
Triarius repaired what was damaged, and fortified Delos.

PART II

COMMENTARIES

5

Commentary

Book of Marvels

Ghosts

Phlegon's first three narratives (Chapters 1–3) tell of persons who die and return to life, or quasi-life, as ghosts. Since human beings normally may proceed from life to death but not from death to life, moving from death to life implies a breakdown in the categories of life and death and in the relationship between them.

Broadly speaking, Greek tradition knows of two kinds of ghost, the disembodied and the embodied. The former are encountered most memorably in the Homeric poems when the ghost of Patroklos comes to Achilleus in a dream-vision (*Iliad* 23.62–108) and when Odysseus visits the realm of the dead (*Odyssey* 11). The sleeping Achilleus tries to embrace his companion, but fails, and the ghost goes underground 'like smoke'. Achilleus exclaims that even in the House of Hades something remains, a 'soul' (ψυχή) and an 'image' (εἴδωλον), but nothing else. Similarly, three times Odysseus tries to embrace the ghost of his mother and three times she flies from his arms 'like a shadow or a dream'. She explains that such is the nature of the dead after they have been cremated and their soul has flown away 'like a dream' (11.204–24).

The embodied ghost, or revenant, can be illustrated by the famous Heros of Temesa. While on their way home from Troy,

Odysseus and his companions stopped at Temesa in Italy, where one of the crew members, Polites, drunkenly raped a local maiden and was stoned to death by the populace. Odysseus and the others continued on their journey, but the ghost (δαίμων) of Polites terrorized the Temesans, attacking and killing young and old. In order to placate him, the priestess of Apollo instructed them to construct a sanctuary and temple for Polites and each year to give him the most beautiful maiden in Temesa; they did so, and his depredations ceased. The practice continued until one day the athlete Euthymos, who had won the boxing contest in the Olympic Games, chanced to come to Temesa at the time of the annual ritual, fell in love with the maiden, and fought Polites for her, driving him out of the land. Polites leapt into the sea and disappeared, and Euthymos married the girl (Pausanias 6.6.7–11); see Joseph Fontenrose, *Python: A Study of Delphic Myth and Its Origins,* Berkeley and Los Angeles 1959, 101–03. Polites's body was obviously as substantial and functional as that of any living person and even more powerful. The ghosts in Phlegon's narratives are all of this type.

On Greek and Roman ghosts and ghost stories see Wendland 1911a; L. Collison Morley, *Greek and Roman Ghost Stories,* Oxford 1912; Winkler; Gauger 231 note 19; D. Felton, 'The Ghost Story in Classical Antiquity', diss., University of North Carolina 1995; and for ghost stories in Greek papyri written around the time of Phlegon, J.R. Morgan, 'On the Fringes of the Canon: A Survey of the Fragments of Ancient Greek Fiction', forthcoming in *Aufstieg und Niedergang der römischen Welt.*

Phlegon was a compiler and so drew his material almost exclusively from earlier published works. Although it is generally agreed that his three ghost narratives were composed several centuries before his time, there is disagreement about who actually composed them. The beginning of his first account is lost, but he attributes his second account to a Hieron of Alexandria or Ephesos and his third to a Peripatetic philosopher named Antisthenes. We know nothing certain about these men, but most likely Phlegon himself accepted the attributions, believing that, as sources went, the authors were probably truthful and certainly sensational.

Now, in fact, none of these accounts is what it claims to be, that is, an honest account of an actual historical event; rather, each is a strange and amazing fiction in the guise of history. Early investigators were convinced that all three compositions were produced by a single, unknown man in the second or first century BC (see Rohde, Wendland 1911b: 9–10, and Mesk). They pointed to similarities in theme and diction in the narratives. In each, the supernatural bursts unexpectedly into a community in one bizarre form or another, prompting its members to respond with fear or awe; a revenant figures in all three stories, and other elements such as public assemblies and oracles and talking heads appear at least twice. But more recent scholars have expressed scepticism about the thesis of single authorship (Janda 347–48, note 39, Brisson 1978: 90–91, Gauger 228–30, note 13).

In any case a more interesting question is not whether the individual accounts were composed by this or that writer about whom we know nothing, but why they were composed at all. One of the documents (Chapter 3) is probably a piece of resistance literature, an attempt to discourage Romans from further aggression in Greek territory. Of the other two, one (Chapter 1) is cast as a letter, and originally the other (Chapter 2) probably had epistolary form as well. The production of fictitious letters of different kinds, especially as school exercises, was a common practice in the late Hellenistic period, and these two narratives may have their origin as exercises on a set theme. One of them (Chapter 1) reads very much like a short story.

On fictitious and forged letters see M. Luther Stirewalt Jr, *Studies in Ancient Greek Epistolography*, Atlanta 1993, 20–42, and for ancient epistolary fiction see Patricia Rosenmeyer, 'The Epistolary Novel,' in *Greek Fiction: The Greek Novel in Context*, J.R. Morgan and Richard Stoneman (eds), London 1994, 146–65, and Niklas Holzberg (ed.), *Der griechische Briefroman: Gattungstypologie und Textanalyse* (Tübingen 1994).

A valuable supplement to our knowledge of Phlegon's ghost stories is provided by Proklos, a Neoplatonic philosopher of the fifth century AD (see Appendix 1). While commenting upon the

Myth of Er in Plato's *Republic*, Proklos recounts a number of instances of a return to life that he in turn has taken from a compilation made by a certain Naumachios of Epeiros: the Aitolian Polykritos died and returned briefly to life nine months later, the Nikopolitan Eurynous regained life after fifteen days and lived for a long time afterwards, Rufus of Philippi recovered his life three days after dying and perished again shortly thereafter, and the Amphipolitan Philinnion died as a young bride, returned to life six months later and died again. Of these stories, that of Polykritos and that of Philinnion, both of which Proklos says were recounted in a series of letters, are found also in Phlegon (Chapters 1-2).

Collections of astonishing returns to life were made by a number of ancient authors (Rohde 338). They do not distinguish between revenants, whom we usually regard as in some sense dead, and persons who have had a near-death experience, nearly dying or briefly dying and presently returning to full life and consciousness, typically with a memory of a striking experience from their period of unconsciousness. Thus both kinds of revivification appear indiscriminately in Proklos's collection, and the same is true of the compilation made by Pliny the Elder (*Natural History* 7.52) in the first century AD, but Phlegon features only revenants. On accounts of near-death experiences see in general Carol Zaleski, *Otherworld Journeys: Accounts of Near-Death Experience in Medieval and Modern Times,* New York and Oxford 1987.

1 Philinnion

The intriguing story of Philinnion is probably the finest in Phlegon's compilation. The principal discussions are Rohde, Wendland 1911b: 5-11, Mesk, Hansen 1980 and 1989.

Part of the story is missing because Phlegon's work survives along with that of two other paradoxographers in a single manuscript that is damaged at both its beginning and end. Since the authors appear in the sequence Phlegon–Apollonios–Antigonos, the first part of Phlegon's work and the final part of Antigonos's work are lost. Happily a brief summary of the complete narrative concerning Philinnion is given in the fifth century AD by Proklos (see Appendix 1), and additional inferences about the missing part of the narrative can be made from the extant portion of Phlegon's text.

The chronology and general sense of the events of the first half of the story are as follows. Philinnion wed Krateros, died shortly thereafter, and was placed in the family tomb. Sometime after this, Machates came from Pella to the house of Philinnion's parents Demostratos and Charito, where he resided in the guest room. We do not know what business he had in Amphipolis or with his hosts. Contrary to the conviction of many scholars, Machates is very unlikely to have had a prior personal acquaintance with Philinnion, for he did not recognize her as the daughter of his hosts, nor was he even aware that their daughter had recently died, which implies that he was not a close friend of the family at all.

About a half-year after her death (14) Philinnion returned as a revenant, making her way nightly to the guest room of her parents' house. On each of three nights she arrived at about the same hour (10) and, except for her parents' interruption on the third night (11–12), passed the night with Machates in his room, leaving before daybreak (6) and returning unnoticed to her tomb. She told Machates that she came to him without her parents' knowledge (7), which was true enough, but she did not inform him that her parents were Demostratos and Charito. Nor did she tell him that she herself had died (10) and that her own dwelling was a tomb. For his part he evidently assumed that she was the daughter of a family in town and that from her erotic desire for him she stole out of her house after dark in order to pass the night with him and left before daybreak in order to be back in her room before her own household arose.

During the first evening the lovers exchanged love-tokens, she giving him a gold ring, which he kept in his room (7), he giving her an iron ring and a gilded wine cup, which she took back with her to her tomb (15). On the second evening the nurse chanced to see the lovers sitting together in Machates's room (1)—the tantalizing point at which our fragment begins—and later that evening Charito spied them sleeping in bed (4–5). Charito's confrontation with Machates took place on the morning of the third day (6–9), and that same evening she and Demostratos burst into the guest room, disturbing their daughter's visit and her mysterious business (11–12).

The idea that the deceased maiden and the houseguest had been engaged to be married is an invention of Johann Wolfgang von Goethe in his fine ballad, *Die Braut von Korinth*, or *The Bride of Corinth*, for which Phlegon's story served as an inspiration. Goethe knew no more about the story of Philinnion than we do; indeed, he knew less. Goethe came upon the story of Philinnion in a contemporary retelling rather than in Phlegon himself, but the text of Phlegon upon which the retelling was based was as incomplete then as it is now; nor did Goethe have access to Proklos's summary of the story and therefore to the details it contains from the missing part of Phlegon's story, for in Goethe's day the text of Proklos lay unpublished. In sum, he drew upon a retelling of Phlegon's fragmentary narrative, which he treated freely, elaborating it into a striking poem of vampirism, paganism and Christianity. Whereas in its present state the ancient narrative does not mention the site of the events, Goethe localizes the action in Corinth, and whereas in Phlegon's text the relationship of Machates to the household he is visiting is obscure, Goethe makes the house guest a youth who had been engaged to wed the daughter of the household, a girl about whose death he has not yet been informed; their fathers had arranged the match. The ballad was composed in 1797 and published in the following year.

The Bride of Corinth is a remarkable instance of the influence of art upon scholarship, for the ballad has so strongly impressed itself on the minds of scholars in German-speaking lands that they often view Phlegon's story with Goethe's eyes. Ludwig Friedländer in his *Darstellungen aus der Sittengeschichte Roms* follows Goethe in localizing Phlegon's story in Corinth rather than in Amphipolis (Rohde 329). In his collection, *Altgriechische Liebesgeschichten, Historien und Schwänke, Griechisch und Deutsch (Bearbeitung und Ergänzungen von Franz John)*, Berlin 1970, Ludwig Radermacher (79) gives the title 'A Dead Woman Visits her Fiancé' to Phlegon's text. The house guest Machates, having been engaged to marry the recently deceased Philinnion, has been spared the knowledge of her death. Other examples could be cited. Because of the inherent interest of the ballad for which the story of Philinnion served as a source and because of the influence of the ballad back upon the perception of the ancient story, I include the text of Goethe's poem in this volume, in a new English translation by Breon Mitchell (Appendix 2).

Phlegon's document refers to a king (18), and Proklos calls him Philip. The Greek city of Amphipolis on the Strymon was captured by Philip II of Macedon in 357 BC, after which it was under Macedonian rule. Philip reigned from 359–36 BC. The dramatic date of the events therefore falls within the twenty-year period 356–36 BC.

1 . . . [the nurse] went to the door. As it has come down to us the composition begins in mid-sentence.

2 to the girl's mother. Although the nurse calls out the names of both parents, she runs to Charito, and indeed it is Charito who replies to the nurse, Charito who checks out her extraordinary claim, and also Charito who confronts Machates on the following morning. The drama is carried by the women.

by divine will. The author hints that the gods may be working behind the scene with their own agenda. The phrase is used repeatedly (2, 6, and 11).

7 The youth was anxious. Paul Wendland (1911a: 34) supposes that Philinnion loved Machates, the son of a guest friend in Pella, but her parents forced her to marry Krateros; since she could not forget her love for Machates, she died of grief shortly after the wedding.

She found no peace in death either, and her spirit haunted her old home in its quest for happiness and love. Josef Mesk (300, note 6) assumes that, since the youth did not recognize his noctural visitor and knew of her only what she herself had told him, Philinnion's love for Machates must have been a secret love and that while she lived she must never have actually laid eyes upon him. But these suppositions strain credulity.

The young man is not aware of his lover's true identity. His embarrassment springs from the general fact that he has been carrying on a covert affair in the house of his hosts and not from the particular fact that his affair is with his hosts' daughter, which would be an outrageous insult to them. She makes her way nightly from the family tomb to the house in which Machates is staying and he knows her only as a local girl who visits him at night. Since she arrives from outside, no connection with Charito and Demostratos would suggest itself to him.

the girl's name was Philinnion. The author gives Macedonian colour to his narration by employing Macedonian or Macedonian-sounding names. The Krateros whom Philinnion marries must be, or must be intended to suggest, the prominent Macedonian military commander Krateros (c.370–21 BC) (Rohde 333), virtually Alexander's second-in-command. The addressee of Hipparchos's missive, Arrhidaios, suggests Philip Arrhidaios (c.358–17 BC), half-brother of Alexander the Great (Rohde 330). And Philinnion herself bears a name resembling that of Phila, second wife of the historical Krateros (Rohde 339), as well as that of Philinna of Larissa, Arrhidaios's mother. The Macedonian names are mixed together with other names—Demostratos, Charito, Hipparchos, Hyllos—that appear to be chosen more or less arbitrarily. This mix of authentic and arbitrary names is consistent with the practice of Greek novelists such as Chariton; see Tomas Hägg, 'The Naming of the Characters in the Romance of Xenophon Ephesius', *Eranos* 69 (1971) 25–59.

Wishing to make the matter credible. Machates substantiates his account of the events as a love-affair by producing a golden ring that the girl gave him as a love-token. Later (15) we learn also of an iron ring that he gave her. The exchange of rings was presumably recounted earlier in the missing portion of the narrative, since the first time Philinnion's gold ring is mentioned it is described as 'the ring, the gold one' (τόν τε δακτύλιον τὸν χρυσοῦν), and the iron ring is similarly referred to as something already familiar to the reader: 'the ring, the iron one' (τὸν δακτύλιον τὸν σιδηροῦν). Philinnion also left behind her breast-band, perhaps inadvertently while dressing.

9 **all were grieving.** The household gives up its restraint and grieves freely. We must assume that at this point the young man finally is informed that the woman who has been visiting him is not alive, for presently we observe him evaluating this possibility, finding it hard to believe that he has been consorting with a dead woman (10); Philinnion, we learn, has been dead nearly six months (14).

11 **for three days.** This visit is her third. On the first evening they exchange lover's gifts, on the second evening the nurse catches a glimpse of them together and on this the third evening Demostratos and Charito burst into the guest room. All doubts that the parents and guest may have harboured about the reality and identity of the ghost are dispelled.

on account of your meddling. The encounter of Philinnion and her parents at this time leads to irreparable harm to the daughter that was unforeseen, and cannot have been foreseen, by her parents. Although their human desire to see their daughter again is understandable, however awkward their method of accomplishing it may be, Philinnion's response is reproachful, for their untimely arrival will, as it turns out, deprive her precisely of what she seeks, a return to life. The programmes of the living and the dead clash.

Her speech suggests questions that the narrative does not answer. Since the dead as a rule remain dead, why has Philinnion exceptionally returned for the present, and why does she have an extraordinary chance at a permanent return to life? Why is her opportunity connected with an apparently unrelated activity (namely, consorting with her parents' guest) and conditional upon an apparently arbitrary term of time (namely, three nights)? And precisely what divine taboo do her parents violate by bursting into the room? These questions remain unanswered, doubtless because part of the desired effect of the text is the creation in its readers of a sense of other-worldly mystery arising from the idea that there exists a largely unseen world that is parallel to ours, a world with its own rules and logic, a world that seems to comprehend us but eludes our own understanding.

As a narrative idea, however, a well-intentioned mortal's interrupting a supernatural being who is engaged in supernatural business, frustrating the mysterious activity with which the being is occupied, is familiar from the Greek mythological tradition. In the *Homeric Hymn to Demeter* (231–81) the goddess Demeter is in the process of rendering immortal an infant boy whose nurse she is, burning away his mortal parts in the fire of the hearth, but when her secret nocturnal treatment is innocently interrupted by the child's concerned mother, the goddess instantly leaves off the procedure and departs, and the child thus remains a mere mortal. Similarly, when Achilleus was an infant, his divine mother Thetis would secretly burn away his mortal flesh in the hearth-fire by night and rub him with ambrosia by day in order that he might become immortal and escape hateful old age, but one night the boy's father Peleus awoke during this procedure, saw his son gasping in the flames, and let out a great cry, whereupon Thetis dropped the screaming baby onto the ground and angrily leapt into the sea, deserting them both (Apollonios of Rhodes *Argonautika* 4.865–79).

12 **she was dead.** The supernatural, which entered the household without warning, now departs just as quickly. Just when their hopes are raised that their daughter is somehow alive, Charito and Demostratos experience her loss a second time, an occasion for stunned disbelief and heart-rending grief.

incredible. A recurrent word, setting the tone and suggesting to readers the attitude that they would have had if they themselves had been there at the time (cf. 16).

reported to me. As the narration shifts from third-person (1–11) to first-person (12–18), readers perceive for the first time that the document is not an impersonal, omniscient narration but an alleged eye-witness report by a local participant. Readers of the original text must have known this much earlier, for the supposed letter presumably began with a salutation such as 'Hipparchos greets Arrhidaios' and some kind of explanatory introduction such as 'I am writing to acquaint you with an extraordinary occurrence'.

One might expect the narrator to recount in more detail the forthcoming events, in which he says he participated, than those at which he was not present, but instead his narration becomes more spare. Probably he lingers more on the earlier episodes because they are more sensational and because, as I show below, they remain closer to the story that serves as his source.

12–3 The scene changes from the private environment of the family home to the public environment of the community as a whole, which now shows its own interest in the event, at present only an unconfirmed rumour.

13 kept in check. The narrator is therefore a local official.

14 by early dawn. The beginning of the fourth and final day of events.

the theatre was full. In early times public meetings in Greek towns and cities were held in the agora or other suitable place, but with the construction of stone theatres in many Greek communities, especially in the Hellenistic period, theatres became the usual place of assembly (e.g., Chariton 1.1.11, 8.7.1); see William A. MacDonald, *The Political Meeting Places of the Greeks*, The Johns Hopkins University Studies in Archaeology 34, Baltimore 1943.

14–5 The accommodations for the dead—placement of the corpse on a couch, or bier (κλίνη), within a vaulted chamber (καμάρα)—are authentically Macedonian (Erwin Rohde, *Der griechische Roman und seine Vorläufer*, 4th edn, Hildesheim 1960, 419, note 2; Wendland 1911b: 10–11). In retelling the story, Proklos speaks carelessly of the investigators' *digging up* Philinnion's grave and finding it empty, whereby he unconsciously assimilates the story to what was, for him, more familiar practice.

15 the first day. The love-tokens, a gold ring from Philinnion and an iron ring and gilded cup from Machates, were exchanged by the lovers during Philinnion's first visit, an occurrence that seems to have been described in the missing part of the letter. It seems odd, however, for Philinnion to acquire an iron ring, since ghosts are often represented as fearing iron; see Mesk 301, note 7, citing Riess, 'Aberglaube', RE 1: 50.

16 **Demostratos's house.** Now the community convinces itself of the truth of the incredible events and joins the household in its belief.

17 **Hyllos.** The seer Hyllos focuses the community response. The pollution must be removed and an attempt made to avert the divine anger that its presence is taken to indicate.

seer . . . augur. By 'seer' (μάντις) the narrator probably refers to Hyllos in his capacity as interpreter of prodigies, for which the more precise term was 'observer of prodigies' (τερατοσκόπος), and by 'augur' (οἰωνοσκόπος) he means his ability to decode messages encoded in the cries and flight of birds. See also the comment below at *Mir.* 2.4.

18 **Machates . . . killed himself.** It is unclear whether Machates, despondent at the sudden loss of his lover, chooses to join her, or whether he kills himself from shock, unable to cope with the revelation that his lover is a dead woman. In either case, persons in traditional story who consort with the dead often run the risk of losing their own lives (Wendland 1911b: 6, note 1; Mesk 301, note 8). For example, in an English ballad, *The Unquiet Grave*, a youth sits and mourns at the grave of his beloved for twelve-month and a day, whereupon the dead girl addresses him, asking why he sits weeping on her grave and will not let her sleep. When he answers that he craves one kiss of her cold lips, she explains that if he kisses her lips, his own time will not be long. See Francis James Child (ed.), *The English and Scottish Popular Ballads*, New York 1956, 2: 234–38.

If you decide. The instructions imply that the supposed author is a local official of some importance who is reporting the matter to a higher official, who in turn may decide to bring the matter to the attention of the king. From Proklos's retelling we infer that the alleged author of the letter is Hipparchos, its addressee Arrhidaios, and the monarch Philip of Macedon.

I may dispatch to you. A device for enhancing the credibility of the narrative: an eye-witness is quite prepared to attest to the truth of the matter.

Farewell. This represents ἔρρωσο (= 'be strong' = Latin *vale*), a common closing formula in Greek letters. Phlegon has copied the fraudulent document word for word into his own collection.

The composer of the document relates some of the events in the first person in order to be able to represent the supposed writer of the letter as an eye-witness and so lend credibility to the events. The official recounts the happenings in chronological sequence, and strictly speaking his point of view is ego-narration with hindsight, since he himself would not have known about the anterior events in the household of Demostratos and Charito as they were happening, but only later, after the matter had become public.

Although the action is clearly and effectively recounted, there is some awkwardness, perhaps not readily noticed, between the virtual omniscience of the epistolographer and his own limited participation in the events. He does not explain (because he cannot) how he himself is so intimately familiar with events inside the residence of Demostratos and Charito—events that precede his own involvement in the affair—that he is able to give a detailed account of the actions and feelings and utterances of the nurse, the parents and the guest, as though he had been present, which he was not. His recasting the entire narration as a personal account of the events has the awkward result that his

familiarity with the events in the private household is unrealisti-
cally intimate and inappropriately detailed for the kind of
document that his narration purports to be, a letter from one
official to another, not a piece of short fiction. However, his
improbably detailed presentation deterred neither the paradoxographer Phlegon nor the philosopher Proklos in their credulity
from accepting the letter as an authentic report of an historical
event.

Since the story of Philinnion is not what it represents itself to
be, a genuine report of an actual event, where did its author get
his story? Did he create a historical fiction or did he adapt a
traditional story that was already in oral circulation? In fact he
seems to have done both, drawing upon an oral story in order to
create a pseudo-historical literary fiction, for the central episodes
of Phlegon's narrative are familiar as the central action of a folktale attested in modern Irish tradition, except that the gender of
the protagonists is reversed, the revenant being male and the
houseguest female (Hansen 1980). In a folktale collected from an
Irish narrator in 1936, a servant girl, sent by the mother of the
house to peep through the keyhole of the bedroom, looked and
saw their lodger Máire (= Mary) with a baby in her arms and a
man sitting at her bedside. She ran to tell her mistress, who
judged correctly that the man was her son. The woman
instructed her servant to tell Máire that it was necessary to store
some things in her room, after which the farmer's wife was
secretly bundled up and carried into the room. That night she
saw her son come and sit down beside the bed. Losing patience
she threw off the clothes on top of her and caught hold of her
son. 'May God help us now, Mother!' he exclaimed, saying that
if she only had waited two hours more, she would have had him
forever. Now he must spend seven years in hell because of her.
See Laurits Bødker, Christina Hole and G. D'Aronco (eds),
European Folk Tales, Copenhagen 1963, 136–42, 221.

In another Irish text, this one recorded in 1944, the servant
girl, sent by the mother, went to the girl's room, looked through
the keyhole since the door was locked, and saw a handsome

young man by the bedside and Máire in bed with a baby at her breast. The girl ran back in terror and cried to her mistress that their lodger was in bed with a baby and there was a gentleman at her bedside; the mistress should come and see them for herself. The woman went and looked through the keyhole, recognized the man as her own son, exclaimed, and drew back in silence. A few days later the servant told Máire that it was necessary to hide something away in the room. But the mother disguised herself in straw and a cloak and had herself carried into the room. At midnight a young man entered, sat down and began to talk with Máire. The mother lost patience, tore off her disguise, ran to her son and embraced him. He cried, 'Oh shame, mother! That's a hateful thing you have done to me.' Had she waited a year and a day, he would have been as well as before, but now he must go back to suffer in hell for seven years more. See Sean O'Sullivan, *Folktales of Ireland*, Chicago 1966, no. 24, 151–64, 270–71.

The plot of the entire folktale, as manifested in the thirty or so texts that have been recorded from oral narrators, can be briefly sketched as follows. Escaping an unhappy marriage or a lustful priest, a young woman finds lodging at a farmhouse. One day she encounters the son of the household, who has died and is damned. On his instructions she lodges in his old room, where he secretly visits her at night. She bears him a child, and when one day she does not arise at usual, the woman of the house sends a maidservant to investigate. She spots the young woman in her room together with the deceased son of the household and quickly reports this sight to her mistress, who confirms the observation and presently conspires with the maidservant to be hidden within some household items and conveyed into the room. When the dead youth pays his next visit, his mother rushes to embrace him, but he reprimands her for her impatience, which has ruined his opportunity to regain his life, for now he must spend seven more years in hell. Although first his mother offers to go in his stead, and then his father, each fails. The young woman now offers, and as she sets out he provides her with a ring that will produce food and drink for her in the otherworld. She succeeds in reaching hell, stays there for the required number of years, and returns just as the man is about to marry. By means of the ring she causes him to remember her and they are wed.

On the folktale, known to folklorists as AT 425J, *Service in Hell to Release Enchanted Husband*, see further Swahn 329–33, Hansen 1980, and Joan N. Radner, ' "The Woman Who Went to Hell": Coded Values in Irish Folk Narrative', *Midwestern Folklore* 15 (1989) 109–17.

In the folktale the heroine marries, the marriage is unhappy, and in time she leaves her husband, eventually arriving at the farmhouse where the affair with the dead man will take place. In Phlegon's story Philinnion marries Krateros, dies shortly after the marriage, and six months later Machates arrives at Philinnion's house, where he enters into an affair with her. In sum, although the roles are distributed somewhat differently in the Greek and Irish texts, there is a common sequence of themes: (1) marriage, (2) termination of marriage and (3) a person's arrival at the house of the deceased son (daughter), where she (he) becomes a lodger. In time (4) the deceased son (daughter) of the household begins secretly visiting the lodger in the guest room at night and (5) they become lovers.

Then comes the central portion of the story, in which the correspondence between the ancient and modern texts is especially close. One day (6) a maidservant, looking into the guest room, spots the two lovers together and (7) rushes to inform her mistress, and presently (8) the mistress peeks in for herself. (9) She now conspires to be present in (or to be summoned to) the guest room for the next visit. At evening when (10) the dead person arrives, (11) the mother, overcome with emotion, exclaims and embraces her child, but (12) the dead child reprimands his (her) mother, explaining that if she (or the parents) had only waited for a certain term (= two hours more/year and a day/three days) and had not thus interfered, he (she) would have regained life, but as it is he (she) must return to death.

Overall, the principal action in the final portion of the modern oral texts, expressed somewhat abstractly, is the deliberation of the family about the next course of action, the journey of the substitute to hell, the return of the substitute from hell to the house of the supernatural lover, and the recognition or verification of the substitute's identity. In Phlegon's narrative there also is a journey, not to hell, but to a tomb; that is, the realm of the dead is expressed by hell in the modern Irish texts and by the family tomb in the ancient Greek narrative. The features in Phlegon's story that answer to the concluding actions in the folktale are (13) the deliberation of the community about what course of action to adopt, (14) the journey of the deliberators to the tomb, (15) the return of the deliberators from the tomb to Philinnion's house and (16) the verification that Philinnion's corpse was there. Although the concluding action is not obviously similar on the surface, the parallelism on an abstract level is striking.

I point out two other interesting correspondences. First, the prominence of rings. The folktale heroine brings with her to hell the magical ring that her lover gives her, just as Philinnion brings with her to her tomb the iron ring that Machates gives her. Second, the final union of the lovers. In the folktale, things end happily and the lovers are wed, but in the pseudo-historical text, things end tragically and the lovers die. So the folktale concludes with a wedding, described or implied, whereas the ancient narrative ends with implied death rites for each of the lovers. The lovers are united in life or in death.

The corresponsion is so extensive and complex that there can be no question that these are forms of the same story. The fact that the revenant is female in the ancient text and male in the modern texts is no obstacle to this conclusion, since variation in gender is not uncommon in oral story. Now, it is extremely unlikely that Irish tradition has borrowed the tale from Phlegon, for as classical authors go Phlegon is relatively inaccessible, not to mention the fact that the beginning of his story is simply lost. On the other hand, nothing at all prevents our supposing that the oral tale may be very old and that the ancient author drew upon an ancient form of the story that closely resembles the present-day folktale. The Hellenistic fabricator must have reworked a traditional story, adapting it to his own quasi-literary purposes, which included casting a local official as an eye-witness to the excitement and his recounting the events as a letter allegedly written by the official. Indeed, the Greek story most deviates from the Irish in the part of the narrative in which the Greek author has worked in an eye-witness to the events, the alleged author of the letter. I conclude that the narrative of Philinnion is a literary adaptation of a traditional oral story that was similar to the Irish folktale of the present day.

I make a number of observations on the basis of this conclusion. First, of the parents it is always the mother, and of the lovers it is always the young woman (regardless of whether she is the lodger or the revenant), that the narrative foregrounds. From the agreement of both the ancient and the modern texts it is apparent that this story is much more about women and their relationships than about men. Second, the mysteries of the supernatural world are no more transparent in the modern tale than in the ancient story. We never learn why, of all deceased persons, the child of this particular family gets an opportunity to return permanently to life, nor why the return is conditional upon the revenant's consorting for a certain period of time with the lodger without disturbance from his (her) parents. The treatment of the boundaries of life and death moreover is strangely fuzzy in this story, especially in the modern texts. Third, the modern texts confirm that the relationship of the revenant and the lodger as lovers is not the result of an earlier connection of some sort between them such as betrothal or unfulfilled love; in fact, the story never clearly explains why these persons become lovers.

And, finally, the genetic relationship of the story of Philinnion and the modern folktale (AT 425J) possesses a more general significance for our understanding of ancient folklore and of ancient literature inspired by folklore. AT 425J is a subtype of AT

425, *The Search for the Lost Husband*, the umbrella term for several clusters of closely related international folktales; see Swahn's standard study and Georgios Megas, 'Amor und Psyche', in *EM* 1: 464–72. Characteristic of this tale-type is a sequence of action that can be summarized broadly as (1) the arrival of a human being at the house of a supernatural (usually enchanted) being, (2) the entry of the two into a marriage-like relationship, (3) the breaking of a stated or unstated taboo, (4) the consequent loss or departure of the supernatural lover, (5) an effort (commonly a search) made by the human lover to regain the supernatural lover and eventually (6) the reunion of the lovers. Usually the lodger and protagonist is female and the supernatural lover is male, wherefore the label *The Search for the Lost Husband*, but the reverse is also found. Most of the principal incidents of AT 425 are present in the Hellenistic literary treatment: (1) the arrival of the human at the household of the supernatural being, (2) their entry into a marriage-like relationship, (3) the breaking of an unstated taboo, and (4) the consequent loss of the supernatural lover. Lacking as such are only the protagonist's stay in the death realm as a surrogate for the other lover and the reunion of the lovers, but the journey to the family tomb, the ring in the tomb and Machates' taking his own life, thereby joining Philinnion in death, suggest that elements (5) and (6), or something like them, were present also in the source story. The story of Philinnion is therefore an instance of folktales of the Cupid and Psyche type and, as it happens, it furnishes our earliest evidence for the existence of such stories. Phlegon was an older contemporary of Apuleius (born *c.*AD 123) and certainly compiled his book of wonders before Apuleius wrote *The Golden Ass*, the novel into which he incorporates his famous telling of the tale of Cupid and Psyche. Moreover, Phlegon's spurious letter is not his own composition but merely a copy of an earlier, presumbly Hellenistic, work. The presence already in ancient tradition—or specifically in Greek tradition, since Apuleius is generally supposed to have adapted a Greek oral tale—of two branches of AT 425, Philinnion (AT

425J) and Cupid and Psyche (AT 425B), implies that this international folktale must be quite old.

2 Polykritos the Aitolarch

This story is far more bizarre than that of Philinnion. A prominent man dies after impregnating his wife, who in time gives birth to a hermaphroditic child. As the community deliberates how to respond to the prodigy, the dead man returns as a revenant, siezes the child, devours it except for its head, and disappears again. The child's head utters a prophecy in verse, interpreting itself as it were, and the people heed its prophecy, which comes true.

1 **Hieron of Alexandria or of Ephesos.** According to Proklos (*Comm. in Platonis Rem Publ.* II, p. 115 Kroll), Hieron of Ephesos and other persons reported these events in letters to King Antigonos and to other friends of theirs (see Appendix 1); on this Hieron see F. Jacoby, 'Hieron (20)', in *RE* 8: 1515; *FGH* 518. Of the apparently original epistolary form of this document Phlegon's text preserves no trace, nor has anything survived of the other letters that Proklos says were addressed to Antigonos, which, if they ever existed, would be as counterfeit as the present narrative is. It seems unlikely that Proklos himself has actually seen other letters on the topic, and probably he is speaking only from inference or from a mention of additional correspondence made by his source.

The identity of the alleged epistolographer Hieron remains uncertain, but King Antigonos is likely to be the Macedonian Antigonos I, surnamed Monophthalmos (reigned 306–01 BC), in which case the dramatic date of the events falls within the period of his rule or possibly a little earlier, if we allow for a retroactive use of the title king for Antigonos (Brisson 1978:

89–101). Antigonos II, surnamed Gonatas (reigned 283–39 BC), has also been proposed (Höfer, in Roscher 3: 2,652).

2 **a certain Polykritos.** The man is unknown outside of this story. See Karl Scherling, 'Polykritos (2)', in *RE* 21: 1759–60, and O. Höfer, in Roscher 3: 2651–2, s.v. Polykritos 2.

Aitolarch. An otherwise unattested office, which may have been similar to that of Boiotarch in Boeotia. In the fifth century BC the Boeotian confederation was divided into eleven regions, each one of which selected one Boiotarch and sixty counsellors for the federal government (Brisson 1978: 92–94); accordingly, a Boiotarch was a member of the more select group of officials, like the members of the United States Senate. Evidently the position serves as an index of the considerable prominence of Polykritos and his family, lending weight to the events that ensue.

Locrian woman. Lokris was divided into two non-contiguous states, western Lokris and eastern Lokris. Of these, western Lokris was a close neighbor of Aitolia, lying to its south-east and sharing a border. Politically, Aitolia gradually encroached on western Lokris so that by the end of the fourth century BC western Lokris had been incorporated into Aitolia and was no longer independent. Because of the proximity of the Aitolians and western Locrians and because of their intertwined political history, Lokris in this narrative probably refers to western Lokris (Brisson 1978: 94–95).

departed from life on the fourth night. Like Philinnion in Chapter 1, the future ghost is a newly-wed who dies an untimely death.

3 **two sets of genitals.** That is, although the narrator does not so label it, the infant is a hermaphrodite.

4 took it to the agora. By proceeding immediately to the agora, or market-place, summoning professional diviners, etc., the family shows that it takes the phenomenon to be a portent (τέρας), and one whose significance is public rather than private (Brisson 1978: 103). So also in Chapter 10, below, the birth of a hermaphrodite at Rome prompts the Senate to order a consultation of the Sibylline Oracles.

Probably arrangements for an assembly are made in the agora, and the actual meeting takes place at a site that is not specified. Chapter 1.14 illustrates the common use of theatres as places for public meetings.

sacrificers and diviners. A 'sacrificer' (θύτης, Latin *extispex*) decoded messages found in the entrails of sacrificial animals, whereas a 'diviner', or 'observer of prodigies' (τερατοσκόπος), was an interpreter of prodigies of any kind; subsequently (6) they are all referred to collectively as 'seers' (μάντεις). See in particular Brisson 1978: 103–04 and in general T.P. Wiseman, *Historiography and Imagination*, Exeter 1994, 49–67.

Some of them declared. The two opinions are not strictly alternatives. One party emphasizes the phenomenon as message; the other as pollution. For the former the main problem is to understand the communication correctly; for the latter, to rid themselves of the pollution properly.

From accounts—historical, legendary and fictional— in Greek and Roman authors it appears that the usual method of the disposal of supposed human monstrosities was drowning (cf. Chapter 25) or burning. A case very similar to the present one arises in the *Alexander Romance*. A Babylonian woman bore a child that had a human head in the upper half of its body, which was stillborn, and animal heads in the lower half, which was alive. She brought the child to Alexander, who

summoned Chaldaean diviners to interpret the prodigy.
After the most skilled diviner revealed the prophetic
significance of the child (it portended the death of
Alexander), he ordered that the child immediately be
burnt (Ps.-Kallisthenes 3.30). In Phlegon's narrative of
Philinnion the seer Hyllos proposed that the body of
the revenant be burnt outside the boundaries of the
city (Chapter 1.17). In Italy hermaphrodites were
frequently drowned; notice also Chapter 25, below, in
which a child born with multiple heads and limbs is
drowned.

It was their classification as something unnatural, as
a portent (τέρας, *prodigium*) of evil, that endangered
hermaphrodites and supposed hermaphrodites. It is
precisely this classification that Diodoros Sikelos in the
first century BC criticizes as incorrect and superstitious.
According to Diodoros, around the beginning of
the Marsian War an Italian living near Rome was
married to a person who proved to be a hermaphrodite
(ἀνδρόγυνος), in the sense of being an adult female
whose sex changed to male by the sudden extrusion of
male genitals. The husband brought the matter before
the Senate, which superstitiously and in accordance
with the advice of Etruscan diviners ordered the person
to be burnt alive. Diodoros comments that this person,
who he says was really not a portent (τέρας) at all and
had the same nature as that of other persons, perished
because of a general ignorance of the ailment. He adds
that shortly thereafter a hermaphrodite in Athens was
similarly burnt alive (Diod. Sik. 32.12). The Marsian,
or Social, War took place in 91–87 BC, so that the
events Diodoros describes occurred not long before he
wrote, c.60–30 BC. The disposal of hermaphrodites by
drowning is frequently mentioned by Livy (27.11.4–6,
27.37.5–7, 31.12.6–10) and by Julius Obsequens in his
Prodigiorum Liber, or *Book of Prodigies* (22, 27a, 32,

34, 36, 47, 48, 50, 53); for a chronological list of prodigies drawn from Livy's work, including books of Livy's history that have not survived, see MacBain 127–35. Only a century later the popular attitude toward hermaphrodites seems to have shifted, for according to Pliny hermaphrodites (*hermaphroditi*), which he says were formerly termed androgynes (*androgyni*), were regarded previously as prodigies but now merely as amusements (*NH* 7.3.34). On ancient prodigies in general see Raymond Bloch, *Les prodiges dans l'antiquité classique*, Paris 1963.

The Greek attitude toward hermaphrodites in ordinary reality contrasts sharply with the positive attitude toward the figure of the hermaphrodite in cult and art. See Marie Delcourt, *Hermaphrodite: Myths and Rites of the Bisexual Figure in Classical Antiquity*, London 1961, and *Hermaphroditea: Recherches sur l'être double promoteur de la fertilité dans le monde classique*, Collection Latomus 86 (1966).

5 **black clothing.** Greek ghosts frequently are described as having black skin and shabby, sometimes dark clothing; see Winkler 160–65.

6 **having appealed.** The ghost has come on his own initiative, having made a successful appeal to the rulers of the dead for a brief leave.

those who are master of things beneath the earth. This reference is the first of several vague allusions to the nether powers, which, in order that they may remain intriguingly mysterious, the author of the narrative does not further explain. In the same spirit the revenant presently says that he is not permitted to let the child be burnt and that he is not permitted to linger there long.

not permitted me to let the child be burnt. The ghost says he appears to them on his own initiative and as an agent of the netherworld gods in order to prevent the burning of the child, a procedure which, for reasons not explained, is contrary to the will of the netherworld powers (nothing is said of the mother, whom it was also proposed to burn). Brisson (1978: 104–06, 108–14) argues that the burning of the child alive would constitute an uncustomary act of violence against it, a means of disposal that in effect classified it as an animal rather than as a human, since monstrous or unpropitious animals might be destroyed by burning.

The apparition speaks against violence, which seduces some of his hearers (and his readers) into expecting him to be a gentle being, and so prepares the way for the shock to come.

impending catastrophe. A second reason why the citizens should hand the child over to him is that their precise behaviour now will, it is claimed, determine whether they will suffer a certain calamity in the future or not. Not only must they give the infant to the spectre, but also they must do so with ritual purity, that is, with trust rather than with fear and with goodwill rather than with angry curses. The revenant hints of terrible destruction, which, if it comes, will presumably be caused by the underworld powers, whom the people will have angered by their present misbehaviour.

in an auspicious manner. That is, 'with words of good omen' (μετ' εὐφημίας), or simply in silence, in order to avoid ritually ill-omened speech.

7 **Now some thought.** As before (4), the community is divided in its opinion into two parties.

8 **if trouble befalls you.** The impatient ghost, who as he says is not permitted to linger among them very long, blames the slow resolve of the people for the immediate action he is about to take and for the catastrophe they

will experience later. Evidently the violence to which the Aitolians force him will recoil on their heads (Brisson 1978: 117).

9 **tore the child limb from limb. The shock.** The ghost's action surprises both onlookers and readers, for not only is it horrible and disgusting but also it appears to be meaningless. The suggestion that the ghost ingests the child in order to take it with him, perhaps to revivify it (Otto Höfer, in Roscher 3: 2,651–52 s.v. Polykritos 2) seems unlikely because the ghost consumes only the body of the child, not its head, and because the dead are not in the business of restoring life. In support of the idea of conveyance via ingestion, however, Brisson points to the conclusion of the story of Publius (Chapter 3), in which a wolf devours the body of Publius, leaving his head, which speaks, explaining *inter alia* that Apollo has sent his servant to Publius and conducted him to the realm of the dead. Brisson's idea that infernal beings are characterized by sarcophagy, various demons being represented as devouring the flesh of the dead in the House of Hades (Brisson 1978: 115–7), is not persuasive in the present context, since the infernal demons in question feast upon the dead, not upon the living, as Polykritos does, and certainly not to transport them.

The ghost acts upon its own nature, which does not and need not make sense in terms of everyday human life. The mystery of the otherworld is part of the pleasure of the story, which, if explained, would be less enjoyably intriguing

10 **unharmed by the stones.** Brisson suggests that Polykritos is unhurt by the stones hurled at him because his body is unsubstantial, a mere shade (1978: 107). But it is characteristic of revenants that they be *embodied* ghosts, more or less indistinguishable in their

substance from living human beings and Phlegon's
revenants clearly fit this description. Philinnion so
resembles an ordinary living woman that her lover is
entirely unaware that she is a ghost, and when she
expires for the second time the community disposes of
her body by burning (Chapter 1), just as when the
revenant Bouplagos dies for the second and last time he
is burnt and interred (Chapter 3). Polykritos himself, as
we see, can tear a human body apart and eat it.
Probably he is unharmed by missiles not because he is
a mere shade but because he is preternaturally strong,
like the famous Heros of Temesa, a revenant who killed
persons of all ages in the region of Temesa until he was
propitiated (Pausanias 6.6.7–11).

suddenly disappeared. His work done, the apparition
returns to the netherworld.

11 **the head of the boy.** The *vital head*, or head that
remains alive after having been separated from its body,
is found as a motif in both mythological and non-
mythological narratives (Thompson, motif E783). On
its appearance in Greek tradition see W. Deonna,
'Orphée et l'oracle de la tête coupée,' *Revue des Études
Grecques* 38 (1925) 44–69, and Joseph Nagy,
'Hierarchy, Heroes, and Heads: Indo-European
Structures in Greek Myth,' in *Approaches to Greek
Myth*, Lowell Edmunds (ed.), Baltimore 1990, 200–38.
Unlike some other vital heads, such as that of the
marvellous singer Orpheus in Greek mythology, the
present one does not derive from a person who in life
was notable for skillful speech or song.

foretelling the future. The infant's head begins by giving
reasons why the folk should not act upon their inten-
tion of sending a delegation to Delphi (vv. 188–93).
First, they are polluted with blood and, second, the
head itself will provide the interpretation they need, so

that external consultation is unnecessary. Presumably their pollution derives from their proposal to burn the hermaphroditic infant, which also led to Polykritos's violence against the child. Being unclean they are not ritually fit to consult Apollo's oracle.

The vital head as speaker of oracles appears also in Phlegon's story of Publius (Chapter 3), below, and is familiar in Greek mythology from the Orpheus legend, for Orpheus's head floated to Lesbos where it gave oracles and later was incorporated into a shrine of Dionysos (Philostratos *Vita Apoll. Tyan.* 4.14). Indeed, the narrative sequence of a *sparagmos*, or violent rending of a body, leading to an oracular vital head is found in all three stories (Höfer, in Roscher 3: 2,652). Some kind of opposition to Apollo also tends to be found, as in the present story, in which the oracular head instructs the folk to listen to it rather than to consult Apollo (Brisson 1978: 119).

the hands you hold in the air. At the moment that the head begins to speak, the assembled citizens are voting by a show of hands on the proposal to send a delegation to Delphi.

in the course of a year. After its preamble the oracle offers its prophecy as such, consisting of a forecast of extensive death and catastrophe followed by a forecast of limited survival. Death will come to most Aitolians and Locrians (vv. 194–206), but, just as the speaker's head has survived death and its limbs are not entirely destroyed, so also the Aitolians and Locrians will not entirely perish (vv. 207–15). That is, the fate of the people will be analogous to that of the infant, the greater part of which has died but whose head survives. For this reason its head should remain in the light above ground and not be buried in darkness and death (vv. 211–12). The oracle concludes with instructions

(vv. 211–15). On the oracle see further Brisson (1978: 120–21).

8 **Athena.** The oracle declares that the souls of the Aitolians and the Locrians will live together 'by the will of Athena,' and the Aitolians should remove to a land and 'people of Athena.' What is Athena's connection with these events?

In Greek legend the Locrians have an old and unhappy connection with Athena, going back to the Trojan War. When the victorious Greeks were storming Troy, Locrian Aias (Ajax) raped the Trojan princess Kassandra, who was clinging as a suppliant to a statue of Athena in her temple. According to a strange tradition that can be pieced together from different authorities (who disagree about the details), when soon after the conclusion of the war the Locrians were suffering from a plague, an oracle instructed them to propitiate Athena by periodically sending to Troy two maidens as suppliants. When the Locrian maidens, who were chosen by lot, arrived at Troy, the Trojans tried to capture them and if they succeeded they burnt them; but if the maidens escaped, they proceeded to the sanctuary of Athena, which they then tended as priestesses. When the maidens died, others were sent to replace them. Eventually the Locrians ceased sending maidens, after which Locrian women gave birth to crippled and monstrous offspring, causing the Locrians to send a delegation to Apollo's oracle at Delphi. When the god reproached them for neglecting Athena, the Locrians asked Antigonos to decide which Locrian city should be responsible for providing the tribute. Antigonos declared that the matter should be determined by lot. See J.G. Frazer, *The Library of Apollodorus*, London 1921, 2: 266–69; Fontenrose 131–37.

The historicity of this unlikely custom, concerning which scholars differ, need not concern us. What is interesting are the points of contact between the story of Polykritos and the tradition of the Locrian maidens (Brisson 1978: 96–98). I mention the following: first, the presence of Lokris and the goddess Athena in some connection; second, the theme of Locrian women giving birth to monstrous children (Polykritos's wife bears a hermaphrodite and Locrian women bear monstrous offspring); third, the idea of burning Locrian women, as though they were monstrous or polluted (the Aitolians propose to burn Polykritos's Locrian wife and the Trojans burn any Locrian maidens they catch); fourth, the consultation of the oracle at Delphi about a prodigy (the Aitolians intend to consult the Delphic oracle about the hermaphrodite and the ghost and the Locrians consult the Delphic oracle about their monstrous offspring); and, fifth, the eventual referral to Antigonos (Antigonos is informed of the events in Aitolia and Antigonos is consulted about the choice of Locrian maidens). The conclusion seems inescapable that the author of the narrative about Polykritos had in mind the tradition of the Locrian maidens when he created his own composition, and worked features of it into his narrative. Accordingly, the choice of a Locrian as mother of the hermaphroditic infant and of Antigonos (whichever Antigonos he may be) as addressee has been influenced not only by the politics of Lokris and Macedonia but also by narrative folklore.

It remains unclear which deities—the nether gods or Athena—are managing the events, and why.

19 **my most dread mother.** The fate of the infant's mother was not reported above, but here the infant's head appears to allude to her death.

24 **expose my head.** The vital head instructs the Aitolians not to inter it but to leave it upon the ground, like an infant exposed by its parents.

12 **in the following year.** This conflict appears to fulfill the prophecy of the seers (4) that the hermaphroditic child portended a breach between Aitolians and Locrians, but in fact the text declares that a war broke out between Aitolians and *Acarnanians*. The presumption that the conflict should be one of Aitolians and Locrians is so strong that in his Latin rendering of the text Alexander Giannini translates the relevant phrase as *inter Aetolos atque Locros* (1965: 185), substituting 'Locrians' for 'Acarnanians.' But the Greek reads 'Acarnanians,' and Acarnanians are not Lokrians. In short, the seers are wrong. What, then, is the real meaning of the prodigy?

The hostilities to which the narrative alludes make a good fit with the events of 313 BC, when Kassandros organized an attack on Aitolia with the aid of the Acarnanians (Akarnania borders Aitolia on the west) and the Epirotes (Epeiros borders Aitolia on the north-west), causing such heavy losses that, according to Diodoros Sikelos (19.74), the terrified Aitolians sought refuge with their wives and children in their least accessible mountainous regions. If these mountains were those that lay to the south, separating Aitolia and western Lokris, the Aitolian flight would be consistent with the injunction of the oracle to 'go to another land, to the people of Athena,' for the Locrians, as we have seen, had a special relationship with Athena, and it would be consistent with the oracular statement that the souls of the Aitolians and the Locrians will live together (Brisson 1978: 99–101).

The inter-mixing of Aitolians with Locrians suggests what the true significance of the hermaphroditic prodigy is. It portends not a breach between Aitolians and Locrians, as the diviners speculate at the time (4), but rather its precise opposite, a conjoining of these two peoples. The seers say that just as the child has been separated from its parents, an Aitolian and a Locrian, so also will a separation arise between Aitolians and Locrians. But this interpretation, so far as it goes, would apply equally to any child of an Aitolian and a Locrian, whether hermaphroditic or not, since it is based upon the relationship of any child to its parents and takes no account at all of the infant's hermaphroditism, the physical peculiarity that prompts the interpretation in the first place. The true meaning of the hermaphroditism, the union of two different genders, is unification within a single body, and it signifies here the union of Aitolian and Locrian. Perhaps this significance explains why Polykritos intervenes in the assembly of Aitolians, for both opinions expressed there are wrong: the child is not an omen of divisiveness, nor should it be burnt.

One thing, then, that might have happened differently if the assembly had given the child to the ghost in the first place is that the union of Aitolians and Locrians might have taken place peacefully rather than violently, for the union of the peoples, however short-lived it may have been, seems to be determined from the first, as the prodigy reveals, but the manner of their union appears to depend upon the behaviour of the assembly in its dealings with the revenant. By not handing over the child auspiciously, the people caused the forthcoming changes to be violent. That much of their future, it seems, lay in their hands.

If the conflict engineered by Kassandros is the one that our author has in mind, the dramatic date of the events is 314–13 BC, and the Antigonos to whom Hieron addresses his letter is therefore Antigonos Monophthalmos. Since, however, the war follows the appearance of the apparition and the oracular head by a year, it is difficult to imagine that the present narrative content was once framed as a letter. Would the supposed epistolographer have postponed reporting the astonishing events to the authorities until after he had ascertained whether the prophecy would be fulfilled? If the original text had the form of a letter, surely it was represented as being written immediately after the supernatural crisis the writer describes, as is the case in Chapter 1, while the excitement is still high. I suggest that in the course of its transmission some writer removed its epistolary trappings and appended a sentence or two as an update to the oracle, showing that a year later the prophecy of bloodshed was fulfilled. The follow-up is notably brief and vague.

As a literary composition the document is generally similar to Chapter 1 (Philinnion) in its sequence of events: the supernatural suddenly erupts in a community, the populace responds in the form of a citizen assembly aided by professional interpreters, the citizens confirm or witness the presence of the supernatural, and the community takes some action.

The narrative of Polykritos also appears to be a literary reworking of a traditional oral story, for there is a parallel, previously unnoticed, to the central event of the present narrative in a similarly strange story found in a work of Philostratos (born AD 170). According to his *Heroikos*, several heroes of the Trojan War are active in the present day as animate, embodied ghosts who occasionally interact with ordinary human beings. In particular Achilleus and Helen now live together as husband and wife on Leuke, the White Isle, in the Black Sea. On one occasion a merchant visited the island, and Achilleus appeared to him, entertained him hospitably, and asked a favour of him, which was to procure for him a certain maiden at Troy. When the surprised merchant enquired why Achilleus wanted a Trojan slave, the hero replied that the girl was born in the same place in which Hektor and his ancestors were born and was of the same blood as Priam. Assuming that the hero was in love with the Trojan maid, the merchant purchased her and sailed back with her to the island. The hero thanked him, rewarded him generously, and told him to leave the girl on the beach when he departed, which the merchant did. As the man sailed away, he and his crew heard the girl's screams as Achilleus tore her apart limb from limb (*Heroikos* 215). Since the story is neither well known nor easily available in translation, I give a rendering in Appendix 3. On the story itself see L. Collison Morley, *Greek and Roman Ghost Stories*, Oxford 1912, 27–32; Graham Anderson, *Philostratus: Biography and Belles Lettres in the Third Century* AD, London 1986, 246–48.

Despite some obvious differences, the stories of Polykritos and Achilleus are both about an encounter between a revenant and a human being (or human beings), and they share an almost identical course of action. The ghost of Polykritos appears to a gathering a people; he asks them to hand over his child to him; when they hesitate, he takes the child himself; the ghost tears the infant limb from limb; the people respond with horror and disgust. Similarly, the ghost of Achilleus appears to a merchant; he asks the man to procure a certain girl for him; the merchant complies; the ghost tears the girl limb from limb; her cries reach the ears of the departing merchant and crewmembers. One could abbreviate the plot sequence as (1) appearance, (2) request, (3) procurement, (4) dismemberment, (5) witnessing.

Clearly the central strategy of this little story is to create surprise and shock. A ghost makes an appearance, seeking out an encounter with a human (or humans). He acts kindly: Polykritos mentions his goodwill and the importance of not burning the child;

Achilleus plays the hospitable host. As it turns out, he wants something that the human can provide. When he makes his desire known, his motivation appears to be ordinary human affection: the father wants his child, the lover desires his beloved. There is, it is true, something extraordinary about the object of desire: the child is a hermaphrodite, the girl is the last vestige of the Trojan royal house. The apparition acquires the object of his apparent affection—and then violently rips it to pieces. We perceive too late that we have been lulled into expecting, or perhaps into wanting, human love to motivate a creature that is only apparently human, a revenant who belongs to another order of being and obeys different rules.

Since the stories of Polykritos's ghost and Achilleus's ghost are not so similar on the surface that one is likely to be a direct reworking of the other (and in any case the document preserved by Phlegon cannot have been inspired by that of Philostratos, which is later), probably both composers drew independently from sources, whether oral or written, that ultimately went back to a traditional ghost story. Let us call this story *The Dissembling Revenant*. To my knowledge, it is not attested elsewhere.

In its Achillean form the story coheres better as a narrative than in its Polykritan form. There is an exquisite ambiguity in the Trojan maiden, for as a maiden she could attract Achilleus's affection, and as a representative of the Trojan royal family she could draw his hostility. The merchant who procures her for the hero assumes the former to be the case, and this assumption proves to be wrong. In Polykritos's narrative, however, there is no finely balanced ambiguity in the relation of the infant to Polykritos, for as Polykritos's offspring the child should attract Polykritos's affection, but there no obvious counterbalance to this factor, and for this reason Polykritos's motive in tearing the child to pieces and eating his body is more puzzling than Achilleus' motive for tearing the maiden limb from limb. The feature of perfectly balanced ambiguity in the infant is expressed, not in a dual relationship of some sort to Polykritos, but in its gender, but there is no obvious connection between the hermaphroditism of the infant and the striking behaviour of the ghost.

As a story *The Dissembling Revenant* is a traditional narrative routine, which I shall call simply a *string*. Another, smaller string in this document is that which leads to the uttering of prophecies by a vital head. This routine is composed of two elements in sequence: dismemberment, oracular head, in association with some kind of opposition to Apollo (Brisson 1978: 119). The fact that these two strings have an unusual feature in common—*sparagmos*, or dismemberment—has facilitated their combination into a single narrative. A third string is the familiar scenario according to which a community responds to a prodigy: appearance of a prodigy (ghost, monstrous offspring, etc.), assembly of citizens, resolution (disposal of the prodigy, purificatory and/or expiatory rites, embassy to Delphi for divine advice, etc). In this case the scenario is recurrent because it probably reflects the reality of actual practice. These strings are some of the important narrative materials that the composer of Chapter 2 has drawn upon, consciously or unconsciously, in his composition.

3 Bouplagos and Publius

This narrative may be treated as consisting of three parts: the prophecies of Bouplagos, the prophecies of Publius, and the frame into which they are placed, amounting to an introduction giving the historical setting, transitions between prophecies and a conclusion. Since Bouplagos dies and briefly returns to life, it is primarily his story that qualifies the composition as a whole for inclusion in a collection of narratives of returns from death, but the story of Publius with its motif of a vital head expresses a somewhat similar idea.

The narrative recounts how the Romans, following a victory over the Seleucid monarch Antiochos, are occupying themselves with burial of their dead and related matters, when a slain enemy officer, Bouplagos, revives on the battlefield, goes to the Roman camp, and utters an oracle to the Romans to the effect that they should cease their looting of the dead; the behaviour of the Romans angers Zeus, who will send an army against them into their own homeland. The frightened Roman commanders send a delegation to Delphi to ask the oracle what they should do, and the priestess similarly advises them to restrain themselves from war in order that their own land not be ravaged by war. Hearing this, the Romans renounce their plans to wage war in Europe. While they are engaged in sacrificing, one of the commanders, Publius, suddenly falls into a state of divine frenzy. He utters oracles, some in verse and some in prose, predicting in various ways that Rome will fall to a powerful army from Asia Minor. Finally he foretells that he himself will be consumed by a wolf, after which a wolf appears and devours him, except for his head, which utters a final prophecy. The Romans return home after erecting a temple on the site to Apollo. Publius's prophecies come to pass.

The composition features a sequence of related events more than a story as such, for the modest element of action serves only as a vehicle for the many prophetic statements that dominate the piece, all warning of dire consequences for the Romans if they should continue their policy of foreign conquest. Internal evidence indicates that some of the oracles must predate the composition of which they are now a part. The document was composed, whether by Antisthenes or someone else, in the second or first century BC, presumably as a piece of resistence literature whose purpose was to deter Romans against further aggression in the Greek-speaking world. In Phlegon's day the political relationship of Greeks and Romans had of course changed greatly, the different Greek-speaking states having become Roman provinces, so that when Phlegon incorporates the document into his collection of *paradoxa* it is not for its now outdated warnings against Roman territorial expansion but for the presence in it of bizarre and sensational themes (Gauger 227), especially that of a return from death to life, which it shares with the preceding two narratives. Thus, whereas the primary interest of the composer probably lay in the prophecies, for which he devised an exciting narrative frame, it was the wonders of the narrative frame that attracted the anthologist Phlegon. All three of Phlegon's ghost narratives recount the sudden and mysterious irruption of the supernatural into the ordinary life of a community, attended by the utterance of prophecies and other striking events.

Phlegon's third story has attracted much attention from scholars. For recent discussions see Gabba 1975, Gauger, Martelli and Peretti.

> 1 **Antisthenes the Peripatetic philosopher.** The identity of this Antisthenes has been much discussed. Although Rohde and Mesk believe that he is entirely fictitious (as also Hieron, the alleged author of the preceding document, may be), other scholars identify him with the Antisthenes who wrote a work on philosophic succession (Φιλοσόφων Διαδοχαί); with Antisthenes the Rhodian historian (*FGH* 508); or as an otherwise unknown author of this name. None of the arguments seems to me decisive. See Janda, Gauger 238–44, Peretti.

> **Thermopylai.** The battle at Thermopylai between Rome and King Antiochos III of Syria took place in 191 BC, which is therefore the dramatic date of the narrative.

> 3 **conspicuous omens.** The omens are the supernatural events that are detailed in the two prophetic episodes of

the document, namely, the temporary return to life of
the slain combatant Bouplagos and the prophecies he
reveals, followed by the inspired state into which the
Roman general, Publius, suddenly falls, with his
prophecies and his strange fate.

Bouplagos

4 **Bouplagos.** Pliny reports a wondrous event of the
Sicilian War (38–36 BC) that closely parallels the
present occurrence. The forces of Pompey took captive
one of Octavian's men, a certain Gabienus, and slit his
throat, almost severing it. A day later the man recovered sufficiently to say that he had been sent back by
the lower powers with a message for Pompey. He
revealed that the gods now favoured Pompey's cause,
and prophesied that things would conclude as Pompey
wished and that, as proof of this, he himself would
expire immediately after having delivered his message.
And so it happened. Pliny cites the narrative as an
instance of a report of a return-to-life coupled with a
prophecy, which he says he himself does not otherwise
include in his work since such narratives are often
untrue, as also this one must be, inasmuch as the
outcome of the conflict did not confirm Gabienus'
message (NH 7.52. 178–79).

Since essentially the same legend is attached both to
Gabienus and to Bouplagos, the story itself is probably
a migratory legend: (a) after a battle in which men die,
(b) one of the slain enemy revives, (c) delivers a message
from the netherworld powers in the form of a
prophecy, (d) and presently expires again. The rhetoric
of the story argues that the oracle should be believed,
for since the speaker is the mouthpiece of the gods and,
being dead, cannot be motivated by personal gain,
there can be no reason to doubt its truth. The story of

Polykritos (Chapter 2, above) might be regarded as a third realization of the type or string, but in a civic rather than in a military setting: (a) as a young man Polykritos unexpectedly dies (as abruptly, one notices, as if he were a soldier fallen in battle), (b) returns to life, (c) delivers a message from the netherworld deities and (d) shortly thereafter returns to death.

a cavalry commander. Like the Aitolarch Polykritos earlier (Chapter 2) and the Roman commander Publius later (section 8, below), Bouplagos is presented as an important official, doubtless to lend weight and credence to the strange story in which he appears.

soft voice. The same expression is used of the speech of the revenant Polykritos (Chapter 2.6).

Stop despoiling. Unlike the friendly message of Gabienus in Pliny's story, that of Bouplagos is hostile to its hearers, although it seems unclear just what Roman behavior so offends Zeus, since there is no manifest reason why Zeus should favour the Syrians as a political entity against the Romans and the Romans themselves are doing only what every other victorious army does after a battle, which is seeing to the dead and the spoils. The prophecy is vague, however, with respect to the particular agent, means, and time of the threatened revenge; see Gauger 249.

Kronides. A patronymic signifying 'son of Kronos'.

5 **cremate.** The men plan to burn the unnatural manifestation, perform a sacrifice and seek professional interpretation. Notice the more or less similar communal responses to prodigious phenomena in the narratives of Philinnion (Chapter 1) and Polykritos (Chapter 2).

6 **Pytho.** That is, Delphi.

the Pythia. The priestess of Apollo's oracle at Delphi.

Restrain yourself. Although the message delivered by the Pythia bears a hostile tone, it is not identical to that conveyed by Bouplagos. Athena, not Zeus, is the deity of revenge, which at least is consistent with the fact that Athena was hostile to the Trojan cause during the Trojan War and so might be expected to be hostile as well to Romans as supposed descendents of the Trojans. Here, moreover, the threatened punishment of the Romans is only conditional, for if the Romans show restraint they may be spared an attack on their own land. Inconsistencies between the oracles are probably the result of their having been composed by different authors at different times. On the present oracle see Parke and Wormell 1: 276–77 and 2: 173–74 (no. 428); Fontenrose 261 (H55); Gauger 249–51.

Pallas. That is, Pallas Athena = Athena.

Ares. A common metaphor for 'war', 'battle', 'slaughter'.

7 **they renounced entirely.** The Romans' case against Antiochos was that he had left his own sphere of influence in Asia and invaded Europe. The present passage represents the Romans as acting out the policy that for his part Antiochos should have desired for them, namely, to restrict their own activities to Italy.

shared temple of the Greeks. No such temple at Naupaktos is known; see Gauger 234.

first fruits. First fruits (ἀπαρχαί), or firstlings, are an old and elemental form of offering to the gods according to which one gives the first portion of something such as meat, grain, wine, or wool, usually in modest quantity; see Burkert 66–68.

Publius

8 **Publius.** Many scholars understand Publius as Publius
Cornelius Scipio, who did accompany his brother
Lucius to Asia Minor as the latter's legate when Lucius
held the command against Antiochos III, shortly after
the battle at Thermopylai in Greece; Lucius subsequently overcame Antiochos at Magnesia (189 BC), and
this may well be the case. But it is also possible that the
narrator, by giving only the *praenomen* of the possessed
man, wishes to avoid clearly identifying him as Scipio
or as any other prominent Roman, for to do so would
make the entire account easily falsifiable, since the
narrative would be plainly inconsistent with the known
facts of the man's life. In either case, in choosing the
name Publius the author wishes at least a thought of
the historical Scipio to pass across the mind of the
reader, suggesting, if not actually portraying, historical
fact in the same spirit perhaps as does the author of the
story of Philinnion (Chapter 1), who creates an atmosphere of historicity in his fiction by employing proper
names that are appropriate to Macedonia and to the
time of Philip. On the question of Publius and Scipio
see Jacoby (*FGH* Comm. 845), Holleaux 306, Janda
343 note 12, Gabba 1975:9, Gauger 233, Peretti 46.

O my country. Publius's prophetic utterance, the first of
several from his mouth, agrees with that of the Pythia
in representing Athena as the angry deity and in using
Ares as a metaphor for war, but the oracle presupposes
a different historical situation from that given in the
narrative frame, for the oracle speaks as if the Romans
had just waged war in Asia Minor (as they later
would), whereas the frame represents the present event
as following immediately upon the battle at
Thermopylai in Greece. The inference is inescapable

that the prophecy was composed for a different context
from that in which it now finds itself. Although in its
details it is less vague than its predecessors, declaring as
it does that a coalition of Asian and European armies
will invade and overcome Italy, the precise identity of
the Eastern and Western powers remains unstated. And
indeed we can only conjecture exactly whom, if
anyone, the author of the prophecy may have had
in mind, since we do not know when the oracle was
originally composed or who composed it. See Gauger
251–55.

Thrinakia. That is, Sicily.

Ausonia. That is, Italy. The Greek text is corrupt here,
'Ausonia' being the editor's conjecture. For other
suggestions see Arthur Ludwig, 'Zu Phlegon Mirab. c.
3', *Rheinisches Museum für Philologie* 41 (1886)
627–28; Morel 172–73; and E. Orth, 'Obeloi',
Philologische Wochenschrift 55 (1935) 109–10.

9 **I reveal.** A *vaticinatio ex eventu*, or prophecy made
after the fact, which, being in prose rather than in
verse, probably was not an anonymous oracle in circulation that the composer has conscripted for his
narrative, but rather a prophecy composed by him for
the present story. See Holleaux 1930, Janda 347–48,
Gauger 255–56.

Ainioi. On the emendation 'Ainioi' for the 'Ainianoi' of
the manuscript see Holleaux 1930.

When the others have come safely through. Here I read
the usual emendation (διασωθέντων 'having come
safely through') in place of Giannini's (δημωθέντων).

11 **When glimmering Nesaian horses.** The prophecy begins
with an *adynaton*, or impossibility, like the colloquial
American expression 'till hell freezes over' = 'never'; see

Archer Taylor, 'Locutions for "Never"', *Romance Philology* 2 (1948–49) 103–34. Referring to a statuary group at Syracuse that represented the sun–god Helios in his chariot driving his steeds, the prophet says that when Helios's horses come to life and walk from their base onto the ground, then also will Rome's troubles be fulfilled (vv. 1–8). The second part of the oracle catalogues the miseries that Rome will suffer in the forthcoming war on her soil (vv. 9–16).

Gauger understands the prophecy to mean that first the wondrous quickening of the horses will occur, whereupon there will come the terrible punishment of Rome. The idea is that, inasmuch as the wonder of the horses will never be realized, the prediction will remain permanently open, and since it cannot become outdated, a hope for its fulfillment is never precluded (Gauger 257–58).

Although it may seem natural to read the order of external events as corresponding to the order of poetic presentation, miracle preceding misery, this reading in fact yields no sense, for then the plain message of the prophecy would be that just as Helios's statuary horses will never step off their pedestal, so also Rome will never suffer retribution. But this cannot be its meaning, unless we are prepared to see in it a message that is inconsistent with, indeed the opposite of, everything else in the entire document, not least of all the relish with which the composer details Rome's future sufferings. The proper sense, I suggest, is that misery precedes miracle. That is, the sequence of events does not correspond to the sequence of poetic presentation but is, as it happens, the reverse of it. War and its terrible consequences will come to Rome, and Rome's miseries will not come to an end until Helios's statuary horses come to life and step down from their pedestal. In short: Rome's sufferings will never cease.

Both readings may be extracted from the oracle because of an ambiguity, surely unintended, in a verb in the eighth verse (τελεῖται: 'will be accomplished, fulfilled, come to an end') that allows the *adynaton* of the Syracusan horses to be understood as signalling either the *onset* or the *end* of Rome's miseries: 'At that time, Rome, your harsh sufferings will all be fulfilled'. Although I retain the ambiguity in my rendering, the prophecy as a whole makes sense only if it is understood to mean: 'At that time, which will never come, your sufferings will finally be over'.

Expressions signifying 'never' or 'forever' and referring to a stable phenomenon (or to its opposite, an inversion of familiar order) are well attested in antiquity. According to Herodotos the Athenians declared that so long as the sun should travel the same course as it then travelled, they would never come to terms with Persia (8.143.2). In a poem of Vergil a shepherd expresses his adoration for a certain youth by saying that the stags will sooner graze in the air, the sea will sooner deposit its fish to live on the shore, and the Parthians and Germans will sooner exchange their countries with each other than that the look of that youth will fade from his heart (*Eclogue* 1.59–64). These expressions are a strong and lively way of denying that some particular thing will ever change.

On the oracle as a whole see Morel 173–74, Gauger 256–59, Peretti 52–53.

Nesaian horses. The Nesaian (or Nisaian) horses, named for the Nesaian Plain in the land of the Medes, are often mentioned appreciatively by ancient authors (e.g., Herodotos 3.160). They were the most famous horses in antiquity, so highly esteemed that Nesaian breeders were said to rear steeds for the sun-god Helios. See R. Hanslik, 'Νισαῖον πεδίον', in *RE* 17: 712–13.

Eetion. The sculptor Eetion is mentioned also by Theokritos (*Anth. Pal.* 6.337); see A. Meineke, 'Kritische Blätter', *Philologus* 14 (1859) 22–24.

He laid. The text of this line is too corrupt for translation.

the son of Hyperion. Helios.

12 **huge red wolf.** The colour red was associated particularly with the dead and the realm of the dead; see Gauger 237–38.

Take . . . as proof. Like Gabienus (see comment on Chapter 2.4, above), Publius suggests to his audience that they employ his final forecast, that of his own death, as an index of reliability for his other predictions.

saying that it would not be to their benefit. Like the ghost of Polykritos (Chapter 2.6), the possessed Publius merely alludes darkly to an evil that will befall the folk if they do not permit him to have his way. Within the story the vagueness of the supernatural being's threat suggests a slight impatience with the ignorance of his non-supernatural hearers; for the reader the hints of another world with other rules create an enjoyable air of mystery.

14 **Touch not my head.** Like the vital head in the preceding narrative (Chapter 2.11), the vital head of Publius addresses the folk, instructing them to leave it unburied and, as Apollo's agent or substitute, foretelling war for them.

To this land. The referent is unclear. Although the scene of Publius's prophecy is Naupaktos in Aitolia, the mention of long walls (v. 7) brings Athens to mind.

15 **Apollo Lykios.** Here the phrase must signify 'Apollo of

the Wolf', referring to the red wolf in its role as servant of Apollo (cf. 14). The similar epithets of Apollo, *Lykios* and *Lykeios*, resembled *inter alia* the place-name *Lykia* 'Lycia' and the noun *lykos* 'wolf' sufficiently to make their specific derivations uncertain even in antiquity. By Phlegon's time they were probably homonyms; see W. Sidney Allen, *Vox Graeca: The Pronunciation of Classical Greek*, 3rd edn, Cambridge 1987, 73.

each person sailed to his own land. As Gauger remarks (235), this happy conclusion is fairytale-like. It is unthinkable that in a context of war a Roman army, moved by prophecies, would simply return to Italy.

Everything foretold. As in the story of Polykritos (Chapter 2), the present narrative follows up the prophecies with a succinct historical comment. But the statement is vague, citing no relevant historical event that actually came to pass.

No explanation is offered for the strange fates that befell Bouplagos and Publius, and we are left to infer that for reasons of their own the gods selected these men to carry important messages to the living.

Sex-Changers and Hermaphrodites

This section consists of seven items having to do with sexual ambiguity. The element of the wondrous lies again in basic categories that become mysteriously fluid. Hermaphrodites and revenants both represent a breakdown of basic dyadic oppositions—male and female, life and death; and both incorporate them in an incomplete way: a hermaphrodite is at once male and female but not fully either, just as a revenant is both alive and dead but belongs completely to neither state.

The entries are a mix of Greek mythological traditions and of narratives set in recent time, from 125 BC to AD 116. Phlegon arranges them in a roughly chronological sequence from the Heroic Age to his own century. An exception is Chapter 10, which comes at the end of the sequence, probably because the kind of hermaphroditism it concerns is synchronic rather than diachronic, that is, a person who manifests both male and female sexual characteristics rather than one who apparently changes sex, and so serves as a transition into Phlegon's next category, human monstrosities.

4 Teiresias

1 **Hesiod.** Phlegon names Hesiod (fr. 275 M–W), Dikaiarchos (fr. 37 Wehrli), Klearchos, and Kallimachos (fr. 576 Pf) as sources for the story. In any particular case his citation can mean either that he read the author at first hand or that he found the author credited as a source at second hand. The tellings cited above have not survived independently, but the story is amply attested in other ancient authors (e.g., Apollodoros *Bibl.* 3.6.7, Ovid *Met.* 3.316–39, Hyginus *Fab.* 75), and the extant accounts differ from Phlegon's only in relatively minor ways, such as what precisely Teiresias does to the snakes and exactly how much greater women's share of sexual pleasure is than men's. The story is also found briefly recounted by the Vatican paradoxographer (31), too briefly, I think, to be comprehended by anyone who is not already acquainted with the story. The ancient texts are conveniently printed, with French translation, in Brisson 1976. On the story see Krappe, Forbes Irving 162–70 and Gantz 528–30.

1–2 **the other . . . the one.** That is, τὸν ἕτερον . . . τὸν ἕνα. Phlegon oddly reverses the usual sequence of the terms, so that instead of Teiresias's wounding first 'the one' and later 'the other,' he wounds first 'the other' and later 'the one.' Brisson (1976: 12) suggests that Phlegon plays on the double sense of ἕτερον, so that it signifies both 'the other (of two)' and also 'the different (one)', that is, the female, the one differing in gender from Teiresias. This explanation is consistent with the few texts (Schol. on Homer *Od.* 10.494 and Eustathios *Comm. ad Hom. Od.* 10.494) that actually specify the gender of the serpents, for according to them Teiresias attacks a female serpent during the first round and a male during the second; accordingly, he changes into a woman after striking a female serpent, and back into a man again after striking a male serpent.

He went from being a man. Depending upon the version of the story, Teiresias kills, wounds, strikes with a stick, or stamps upon one or both copulating serpents (Brisson 1976: 24). Regardless of the act, the result is the same: he is supernaturally transformed into a woman. The reason is not obvious why his behaviour should have such a consequence and none of the ancient texts ventures to explain it. For modern attempts to understand the episode, see especially Krappe, Brisson 1976 and Forbes Irving.

It seems to be insufficiently appreciated, however, that the basic events of the Teiresias story closely match those of an international folktale, according to which a man who is engaged in a certain activity or comes to a certain place is changed into a woman, in which state the protagonist lives for seven years as a married woman and bears seven children. When subsequently he engages in the same activity or comes to the same place in which the original transformation took place, he becomes a man once again. Returning home he learns from his wife that he has been absent only a few moments. See Michio Sato, 'Geschlechtswechsel', in *EM* 5: 1,140 for an account of this folktale in particular, and 5: 1,138–42 for change of sex as a theme of traditional oral story in general. I suggest that the legend of Teiresias is a mythologization of the international tale in its ancient form.

2 **the creatures.** Except of course for the few versions in which Teiresias kills a snake in each encounter, the texts usually imply that in the second encounter Teiresias comes upon the same two creatures engaged in the same activity at the same site.

recovered his former nature. Greek and Roman stories of sexual transformation ultimately involve a change from female to male; the few instances of a change from male to female, as in Teiresias's first metamorphosis, are only temporary. An exception of sorts is Hermaphroditos, a son of Hermes and Aphrodite, a youth who became a hermaphrodite after coalescing physically and against his will with the aggressively amorous nymph Salmacis (Ovid *Met.* 4.285–388); however, according to a different version of his story he was born a hermaphrodite (Diodoros Sikelos 4.6.5).

3 **Zeus and Hera had a quarrel.** The domestic quarrelling of the king and queen of the Olympian gods, attested as early as the first book of Homer's *Iliad* (1.533–600), is a commonplace of Greek mythology.

nine tenths. Most versions agree that the allotment of sexual pleasure is $1/10$th for men and $9/10$ths for women, and all agree that women's share is the greater. The Greeks generally believed that women were more prone than men to having sex because women were less able to control their desires; see Roger Just, *Women in Athenian Law and Life*, London and New York 1991, 157–65. The notion of an unequal distribution of sexual pleasure between men and women might constitute one idea for why this was so.

4 Hera angrily gouged out his eyes. In a rival version of Teiresias's blinding and acquisition of prophetic gifts, the youth accidentally comes upon Athena bathing, whereupon the angry goddess tears out his eyes, giving him in compensation the power of divination (e.g., Kallimachos *Hymn* 5.75–136, Apollodoros *Bibl.* 3.6.7). What the two traditions have in common is the idea of a male intrusion upon the intimacies of women: the young male Teiresias, by passing a period a time as a woman or by seeing a goddess naked, is an involuntary spy who comes into the possession of information that it is not proper for him to have (Forbes Irving 167). The logic of blinding as a response is clear in the case of Athena, since she removes the offending organs of sight, but in both traditions we may understand blinding to function as a kind of emasculation of Teiresias. See further G. Devereux, 'The Self-blinding of Oidipous in Sophokles: *Oidipous Tyrannos*', *Journal of Hellenic Studies* 93 (1973) 36–49, esp. 40–46.

gift of prophecy. As often in mythology, a special gift balances a loss of some sort, as in the legend of Kainis (Chapter 5, below), whose sexual transformation compensates her for her involuntary sexual encounter with Poseidon.

seven generations. Nearly all sources agree on Teiresias's longevity, which as here is usually described as a lifetime of seven generations. For the association of prophets and longevity, notice the long-lived Sibyl of Erythrai, who according to Phlegon (*Mac.* 2–4) lived about a thousand years.

5 Kainis

A second mythological tradition concerns Kainis, whom the god Poseidon changed from a woman to a man. Phlegon cites the same authorities as for the foregoing story: Hesiod (fr. 87 M–W), Kallimachos (fr. 577 Pf), Dikaiarchos (fr. 38 Wehrli).

As usual in ancient stories of a change of sex, the metamorphosis is from female to male. Even for Teiresias (Chapter 4), who undergoes two successive changes of sex, the final state is that of male, and similarly Zeus, who transforms himself briefly into the form of the goddess Artemis in order to gain access to the nymph Kallisto, to whom he is sexually attracted, eventually resumes and remains in his original male form; for the story and its variations see Gantz 725–29.

A change of gender prompts a change of name, in this case a modification of the grammatically feminine Kainis to the masculine Kaineus. Phlegon truncates the legend, giving only the beginning of the story, which features the theme of a sudden change of sex. In the continuation Kaineus becomes king of the Lapiths and a powerful hero. He sets his spear up and either worships it or orders others to do so, but this behaviour angers Zeus, who sends the centaurs against him. Since he cannot be wounded, they overcome him by driving him into the earth. So Kainis becomes not merely a man but even a warrior, a man in the extreme as it were, like the sex-shifter Heraïs, who goes from woman to man to soldier (see the commentary on Chapter 9).

On the sources of the Kainis/Kaineus legend see Roscher 2: 894–97 and Gantz 280–81, and for discussions see John Theoph. Kakridis, 'Caeneus', *Classical Review* 61 (1947) 77–80, and Forbes Irving 155–62. On the theme of sex-change in Greek mythology generally see Forbes Irving 149–70.

6 An Unnamed Maiden

This dramatic narrative initiates a series of four non-mythological accounts of sudden sex-change in human beings from female to male. Told of otherwise ordinary persons, the stories are set in relatively recent times rather than in the mythological past.

The narrative of the maiden of Antioch is both striking and mysterious, the former because the girl's involuntary metamorphosis is explosive, the latter because the transformation is unmotivated and unexplained. It is not represented as being the consequence of something she has done, as in the case of Teiresias, or of something she has experienced, as in the case of Kainis; rather, it just happens. Male genitals suddenly extrude from her, and, as Phlegon says, she becomes a man.

The present event took place in AD 45, as the names of the magistrates named by Phlegon indicate. Reference to eponymous years was a frequent means of absolute dating in antiquity. In Greece the most common practice was to cite the Athenian archon for the year; in Rome, the two consuls. As in the use of Olympiads, the system depended upon the availability of lists. See E.J. Bickerman, *Chronology of the Ancient World*, Ithaca 1968, 67–70.

> **1 hermaphrodite.** According to Pliny, the Greek word 'androgyne' (ἀνδρόγυνος, Latin *androgynus*), that is, 'man-woman,' is the older of two terms in Greek and Latin for hermaphrodite; later authors favored the Greek word 'hermaphrodite' (Ἑρμαφρόδιτος, Latin *Hermaphroditus*) (Pliny *NH* 7.3.34, 11.109.262). However that may be, Phlegon, writing in the century after Pliny, uses only the former term, which he employs in two senses. In Chapter 6–8 it means a human being who is successively female and male (this significance of the word is not recognized in Liddell-Scott-Jones); in Chapter 10 it means a person who is simultaneously male and female. In reality this latter is sexually ambiguous, manifestly possessing the sexual organs of both sexes in an incomplete form; see John Money, 'Sexual Dimorphism and Homosexual Gender Identity,' in *Perspectives on Human Sexuality: Psychological, Social and Cultural Research Findings*, Nathaniel N. Wagner (ed.), New York 1974, 42–79, at 67–68.

4 **Capitoline.** The hill upon which a prominent temple of Jupiter stands. 'Jupiter the Averter of Evil' renders Phlegon's 'Zeus Alexikakos'; for the Greek epithet see C.F.H. Bruchmann, *apud* Roscher 7: 124. It is uncertain what the Latin equivalent is.

No execution or exile is mentioned for this person or for the persons in the accounts that follow.

7 Philotis

In Italy in AD 53, a few years after the experience of the unnamed maiden in Antioch, another girl is mysteriously and unaccountably metamorphosed from maiden to man just before her marriage. The story, recounted tersely and undramatically, is essentially the same as the preceding, and Phlegon's source is perhaps the same for both narratives.

8 Sympherousa

> **hermaphrodite.** We are not told when Sympherousa's transformation occurs; however, Philodemos of Gadara, an Epicurean philosopher of the first century BC, probably has Sympherousa/Sympheron in mind when in illustration of the idea that some things occur infrequently he alludes to 'the person in Epidauros who married as a maiden but then became a man' (*De Signis* 4 De Lacy). If so, the report, for which Phlegon offers no date, interrupts the chronological sequence, for it must have occurred no later than the time of Philodemos.

> **Sympherousa.** Sympherousa and Sympheron are respectively the grammatically feminine and masculine forms of the same name, a Greek participle signifying 'useful'.

9 Aitete

Since Aitete is a married woman, her experience deviates from the pattern of the onset of sudden sex-change just before mating. The event is dated AD 116, in Phlegon's own century, and Phlegon adds, presumably to lend credence to his report, that he himself has seen the person. In the preceding century Pliny similarly says that he personally saw in Africa a certain Lucius Constitius, a citizen of Thysdritum, who had turned into a male on her/his wedding day (*NH* 7.4.36).

Phlegon draws most of his wonders from written works, but if we take him at his word when he says he has seen Aitetos, he is likely in this case to have acquired his information about Aitete/Aitetos in conversation with a living contemporary, either Aitetos himself or a local informant, rather than from a book. He does not describe where and under what circumstances he saw Aitetos, and of course verifying the existence of someone associated with a marvel does not in itself confirm the veracity of the report.

Cases of wondrous sexual transformation, presented in Chapters 6–9, are reported not only by Phlegon but also by Diodoros Sikelos in the first century BC and by the elder Pliny in the first century AD. According to Diodoros, when Alexander the Great consulted an oracle of Apollo in Cilicia, the god told him 'to beware of the place that had borne the biformed one'. The point of the enigmatic message was perceived only later. In Abai in Arabia a local woman named Heraïs, daughter of a Macedonian father and an Arabian mother, married a man named Samiades. A year after they were wed, Samiades departed on a long journey, and Heraïs was struck by a strange and incredible malady. A tumour appeared on her lower abdomen and continued to grow, while at the same time she suffered from a high fever. Doctors were summoned, and they treated her as well as they could. On the seventh day the tumour burst, and a male genital organ together with testicles protruded from her groin.

Since only her mother and maidservants were present at the time, they chose to keep the matter secret, and Heraïs continued wearing female clothing. When however Samiades returned and wished to have sexual intercourse with his wife, she was ashamed to be seen by him, and in turn this behaviour of hers made him angry. The dispute grew to be one between the woman's husband, who wanted his wife back, and her father, who did not support his son-in-law's demand but was ashamed to reveal the reason, so that eventually Samiades was forced to file suit for the return of his own wife. When the judges decided that the woman ought to go home with her husband, she disrobed, revealed her maleness to all, and asked them dramatically whether they intended to force a man to live with a man. Everyone was amazed at the marvel. Doctors, concluding that the male organ had been abnormally encased within the female organ and concealed by a membrane, performed minor surgery to complete the transformation. Thereafter Heraïs wore male clothing, adopted the name Diophantos, and even fought in the cavalry under Alexander. When later King Alexander was murdered at Abai, the birthplace of the biformed one, the sense of the unclear oracle emerged. Samiades, who felt love for his former wife but shame for his unnatural marriage, made Diophantos his heir and then took his own life. So she who had been born a woman acquired the courage of a man, whereas the husband became weaker in spirit than a woman (Diodoros Sik. 32.10.2–9). Diodoros's narrative and that of Ps.-Kallisthenes concerning the Babylonian woman (see the commentary on Chapter 2, above), clearly are variants of the same legend, which recounts how the birth of a biformed child (a mix of male and female or a mix of human and animal) signalled the death of Alexander the Great.

Diodoros reports in considerable physiological detail another change of sex that took place in Epidauros some thirty years later. Kallo, an Epidaurian orphan, seemed to be a girl, although she had an imperforate vagina. When she reached marriageable age she wed a male citizen of Epidauros, but inasmuch as she was incapable of sexual intercourse as a woman she was obliged to submit to anal intercourse. After a time a tumour appeared on her genitalia and caused her great pain. Many physicians were summoned, but the only man who was willing to treat her was a certain apothecary, who made an incision in the swollen area, out of which there emerged the genitals of a man, specifically, testicles and an imperforate penis. When the apothecary had completed the operation he asked for double fee, saying that he had received an unwell woman and made her into a healthy young man. Kallo turned away from her loom and other women's work, adopted the clothes of a man, and modified her name to Kallon (22.11.1–4).

According to Pliny, in 171 BC a girl at Casinum changed into a boy and by order of the augurs was transported to an uninhabited island. He says furthermore that Licinius Mucianus recounted that he had seen in Argos a man named Areskon, whose name had been Areskousa (the feminine form of the same word); she had married a husband but, after developing a beard and other masculine features, took a wife. Pliny adds that he himself saw in Africa a certain Lucius Constitius, a citizen of Thysdritum, who had become a male on his wedding day (*NH* 7.4.36). These marvels of Pliny are later quoted with relish by Aulus Gellius in his *Attic Nights* (9.4.15). Livy also mentions that, among the many other notable prodigies and marvels that occurred in Italy in the year 214 BC. such as a rain of chalk and a talking ox, in Spoletium a woman changed into a man (24.10.6–13), and Augustine probably has this passage in mind in his catalogue of astonishing but harmless marvels that were said to have occurred in pre-Christian times (*De Civitate Dei* 3.31).

In these narratives a female typically experiences a sudden and mysterious metamorphosis of female to male when latent male genitalia burst out of her with little warning. Generally the protagonist is a betrothed maiden, who undergoes the transformation just before her wedding, or a married woman whose transformation occurs sometime in the course of her marriage. In the case of the maidens, the change of sex presumably sabotages the marriage arrangment; in that of the married women, it brings about the end of the marriage.

How something very like these reported transformations can actually happen is illustrated in the well-documented case of a French hermaphrodite, Herculine Barbin. Born in 1838, Adélaïde Herculine Barbin was registered in the civil records as a girl, attended schools for girls, eventually obtained a teaching certificate, and found employment as an instructor in a boarding school for girls. When she was twenty-two years old she began to experience sharp pains in her left groin, which led to her being examined by a doctor. He discovered in her a mix of female and male physical features, namely, a somewhat hairy body, a lack of breasts, male hips, a small imperforate penis that resembled a large clitoris, apparent labia majora that really were underdeveloped testicles, a feminine urethral opening, and a quasi-vagina two inches long that ended in a cul-de-sac. She had never menstruated. The doctor inferred that the pains she was experiencing were caused by 'the belated passage of the testicle through the abdominal ring' (Barbin 126). His patient was, he concluded, a hermaphrodite but with a 'predominance of masculine sexual characteristics,' for which reason the doctor arranged for her to be reclassified in the civil records as a male. Adélaïde Herculine Barbin was renamed Abel Barbin and lived the rest of his short life as a man. He moved to Paris, where at age thirty he committed suicide, leaving behind a written account of his life (see Barbin). Many other cases of this sort could be cited.

In cases of so-called male pseudo-hermaphroditism, then, an infant can be sexually ambiguous at birth or appear to be biologically female. Its parents assign its apparent sex to it, rearing it as a boy or as a girl, but at a later period the supposedly female child experiences masculinization, as Barbin did, precipitating a crisis in sexual identity. See John Money, Joan G. Hampson and John L. Hampson, 'Hermaphroditism: Recommendations Concerning Assignment of Sex, Change of Sex, and Psychologic Management', *Bulletin of the Johns Hopkins Hospital* 97 (1955) 284–300; Garland 128–32.

An apparent change of sex at puberty can also be caused by still another form of male pseudo-hermaphroditism. Several modern communities (e.g., rural Dominican Republic, Sambia of Papua New Guinea) experience a high incidence of male pseudo-hermaphroditism as a result of a genetic deficiency that controls the prenatal masculinization of external genitalia. Although they are genetically male, such infants at birth are sexually ambiguous, their external genitalia appearing more to be female than male; however, in late puberty masculinization takes place because of normal plasma testosterone circulation so that male external genitalia become more developed and secondary sexual characteristics appear (deepening of the voice, growth of bodily and facial hair, etc.), though the persons so afflicted still tend to be androgynous in appearance. Since the communities are aware of the phenomenon, infants are sometimes identified as pseudo-hermaphroditic and raised as males in anticipation of later virilization, but some newborns are not so identified, with the result that they are raised as females and at puberty must change to male dress and adopt a male name. See Gilbert Herdt, 'Mistaken Identity: 5-Alpha-Reductase Hermaphroditism and Biological Reductionism in Sexual Identity Reconsidered', *American Anthropologist* 92 (1990) 433–46.

The ancient historical narratives reflect the physical realities of hermaphroditism, but simplify them. The authors generally speak only of the addition of male genitalia to a female, or rather the extrusion of male genitalia that presumably were latent, making no mention of the persistence or loss of the female characteristics that the supposed female presumably has exhibited up to this point in her life, or they speak simply of a change from female to male. Either way the transformation is represented as a change from one discrete sex to another rather than a change to or from hermaphroditic ambiguity. I suggest that there are two reasons for this. First, the change from maiden to young man may *seem* to many persons to be a sudden, radical metamorphosis of female to male. One day she wears female attire and has a female name, and the next day he dresses as a male and now bears a male name. Second, the narratives undergo folklorization, being simplified and intensified to achieve a striking and memorable effect. In the case of the ancient maidens whose transformations occur just before their wedding, the dramatic timing of the event must be determined less by historical reality than by the desire of narrators for narrative effect, for the dramatic timing of the metamorphosis strains credulity.

The transformations are oddly reminiscent of the notion of the development of sex held by the Greek medical writer Galen of Pergamon (AD 129–99), a younger contemporary of Phlegon. In his work *On the Usefulness of the Parts of the Body* he declares that male and female genitals are morphologically identical but inverse. If, so to speak, you turn a woman's genital organs inside out, you will get a man, and vice versa. The crucial factor in the determination of the sex of a fetus is heat. Males produce more heat than females, causing the vagina to pop out as a penis, whereas a defect of heat in females prevents this from happening, resulting in a less perfect being (Galen *De Usu Partium* 14.2.296–99). See further Thomas Laqueur, 'Orgasm, Generation, and the Politics of Reproductive Biology', *Representations* 14 (1986) 1–41.

The pattern of sexual change in the narratives is notably unidirectional: females become males, but males never become females, except in mythological narratives and then only temporarily. In the hierarchy of the sexes in ancient thought, this direction of change is an improvement; see Garland 170–74. When the apothecary in Diodoros's story had completed his surgery upon Kallo, he requested a double fee, saying that he had taken an unwell woman and made her into a healthy young man. That is, just as it is better to be well than sick, it is better to be a male than female. Two stories, those of Kainis/Kaineus and Heraïs/Diophantos, go even further, for the woman becomes not just a man but a warrior, a superman. As Forbes Irving (158) puts it, she is transformed from something less than a man to something more than a man. The hierarchy of the sexes has enjoyed a

long life. In the view of the French medical writer Ambroise Paré
(c.1510–1590),

> it is not fabulous that some women have been changed into
> men: but you shall finde in no history men that have degener-
> ated into women; for nature alwaies intends and goes from the
> imperfect to the more perfect, but not basely from the more
> perfect to the imperfect.

See Jones and Stallybrass 84, quoting *The Workes of Ambrose
Parey*, trans. Thomas Johnson, London 1634, 975, and, more
fully, Ambroise Paré, *On Monsters and Marvels*, trans. Janis L.
Pallister, Chicago and London 1982, 31–33.

The most important difference between the historical and
mythological texts lies in the presence or absence of a cause for
the change. Teiresias undergoes his transformation because of
something he does, and Kainis because of something she suffers,
so that the transformation is a result of an experience. But in the
historical narratives the transformation is not the result of
anything; it just happens, a powerful event that has no apparent
meaning at all.

10 Sibylline Oracles

The final entry in the series of hermaphrodites concerns not
sexual transformation but physical bisexuality, and the emphasis
is not on the hermaphroditic person but on the official response
to the birth of a hermaphrodite, the discovery of whom prompts
the Roman Senate to order a consultation of the Sibylline oracles.
Phlegon's text consists of a brief historical orientation followed
by two lengthy oracles that give instructions concerning the ritual
propitiation of the gods. For the oracles see Diels, den Boer
103–18, MacBain 127–35 and Doria. On Sibyls and Sibylline
prophecy in general see Parke and Potter.

Diels argues that the first and second Sibylline oracles were
composed in 207 BC and 200 BC, respectively, in order that they
might be consulted concerning the appearance of prodigies

during those years; they were then used for a second time when the Decemviri consulted them for the hermaphrodite discovered in 125 BC. Their acrostic composition (see below) indicates in any case that they are unlikely to be older than the Hellenistic period, when acrostics of this kind are first attested in Greek poetry. Because the two oracles are very similar in style and diction Diels believes they were composed by the same person, a Romanized Greek or a bilingual Roman. More recently MacBain and Doria, who in separate studies examine the changes that occur over time in the Roman expiatory ritual for hermaphrodites, argue for a later date of composition, MacBain for 133 BC (MacBain 135) and Doria for 83 BC (Doria 286–88). There is general agreement that in Italy the popular anxiety about prodigies was greater in times of political tension and that the expiatory rites themselves could carry political messages.

1 **A hermaphrodite.** That is, androgyne (ἀνδρόγυνος). The Sibyl is represented as foretelling the birth of the hermaphrodite, which in this text refers to a being whose androgyny is synchronically manifest, as in Chapter 2, rather than covert and/or realized diachronically, as in Chapters 4–9.

consuls in Rome. The event, for which there is no independent confirmation, can be dated to 125 BC by the names of the consuls.

the Senate decreed that the priests should read the Sibylline oracles. We hear in fact of not just one Sibyl but of up to ten different Sibyls, and many collections of oracles were in circulation as the prophecies of this or that Sibyl. They might be consulted by whoever happened to get hold of them, with the exception of those of the Cumaean Sibyl, whose oracles the Roman state guarded and kept secret, regarding them as especially sacred. These might be read only by a special college of priests, and then only upon the order of the

Senate. In 125 BC the priestly college consisted of ten men, the *Decemviri Sacris Faciundis*. The Sibylline oracles were thought to be the very ones that Tarquin the Proud had purchased centuries earlier from the Sibyl of Cumae herself. According to the well-known legend a woman once appeared before the king, offering to sell him nine (or three) books for a certain price, but Tarquin spurned the offer, whereupon she burned three (one) of the books and asked the same price for the remaining books. When he laughed at her, she burned three (one) more and persevered in demanding the same price. Amazed the king purchased what remained (Dionysios of Halikarnassos *Antiquitates Romanae* 4.62; Pliny *NH* 13.27.88; Lactantius *Inst.* 1.6.10–11; Servius *Aen.* 6.72).

1–2 The prose preface to the oracles is so brief and matter-of-fact that it possibly is a rendering of a Latin archival notation serving to index the oracles.

2 **The oracles.** The oracles are in Greek hexameters, the usual form of Greek oracles in folklore and literature. They are difficult to understand and to translate because of the deliberate obscurity of the original compositions, which is made worse by the loss of many lines and the unsound state of the text; however, their basic message is usually clear, a series of instructions for the propitiation of various gods. I do not attempt to capture the obscurity of the originals, which would result in unreadable texts.

The oracles appear to be genuine Sibylline oracles in the sense that they seem to be the actual oracles consulted by the college of priests in 125 BC upon the instruction of the Roman Senate. One can only conjecture how they came to be in circulation. Diels speculates that they were published after the official consultation of 125 BC in order to calm the public by showing how the Sibyl had foreseen the prodigy and also had prescribed a remedy for the gods' anger.

First Oracle

The oracle prescribes rituals for Demeter and Persephone and perhaps for Zeus and Hera, and emphasizes the participation of females, who are divided into age groups (Doria 36).

1a The fate of mortals. Although the first verse of the first oracle is missing in Phlegon's text, it can be approximately reconstituted because Sibylline oracles were acrostics (Greek ἀκροστιχίς), a feature that I do not attempt to reproduce in the English rendering. The first letter of each successive verse, when they are taken together, form a verse, and this verse is identical with the initial line of the oracle.

According to Dionysios of Halikarnassos, citing Varro, after the burning of the Capitol in 83 BC, in which the official collection of Sibylline oracles was lost, the Romans attempted to reconstruct the oracles. They consulted official and private copies of the oracle collections found in Erythrai and other Italian towns, and because of the acrostics of genuine Sibylline oracles they were able to detect a number of interpolations (4.62). Presumably the primary function of the acrostic feature was just this, to encode the oracle in such a way that falsifications, interpolations, and deletions might be more difficult to make and easier to detect, but the acrostic architecture probably also added a mystical air to the oracle and of course gave poetic pleasure in accordance with the aesthetics of the age. In his *De divinatione* Cicero states that in Sibylline oracles the initial letter of successive lines of verse restates the first line of verse, a feature that suggests to him that such oracles are conscious literary products and not verse

produced in a state of divine frenzy (2.54.111–12); for
the supposed frenzy of the Sibyl in her prophetic state,
see Fontenrose 204–12. Since acrostics, concrete
poetry, and other whimsical and virtuosic forms were
fashionable in learned Hellenistic literary circles, the
present oracles are likely to date from this period.

If our oracle were intact, the first verse would be a
line consisting of about forty letters, and the entire
oracle would then be a poem of forty lines, the successive lines beginning in such a way that the first verse
could be read both horizontally and vertically. The
device can be illustrated as follows:

ΜΟΙΡΑΝ ΟΠΙΣΘΟΜΑΘΩΝ ΤΙΝ ΕΦΥ ΠΑΣ ΕΙΣ ΤΟΠΟΝ ΕΛΘΕΙΝ
ΟΣΣΑ ΤΕΡΑ ΤΕ ΚΑΙ ΟΣΣΑ ΠΑΘΗΜΑΤΑ ΔΑΙΜΟΝΟΣ ΑΙΣΗΣ
ΙΣΤΟΣ ΕΜΟΣ ΛΥΣΕΙ ΤΑΔ ΕΝΙ ΦΡΕΣΙΝ ΑΙ ΚΕ ΝΟΗΣΗΙΣ
ΡΩΜΗΙ ΕΗΙ ΠΙΣΥΝΟΣ ΚΑΙ ΤΟΙ ΠΟΤΕ ΦΗΜΙ ΓΥΝΑΙΚΑ
ΑΝΔΡΟΓΥΝΟΝ ΤΕΞΕΣΘΑΙ ΕΧΟΝΤΑ ΠΕΡ ΑΡΣΕΝΑ ΠΑΝΤΑ
ΝΗΠΙΑΧΟΙ Θ ΟΣΑ ΘΗΛΥΤΕΡΑΙ ΦΑΙΝΟΥΣΙ ΓΥΝΑΙΚΕΣ

The first five lines of the oracle are printed here as
upper-case letters and divided into words without
punctuation. The text begins with ΜΟΙΡΑΝ ('fate'),
which can be read horizontally as the first word of the
first line and also vertically as the initial letters in the
first six lines of text. So it continues for forty lines, or
rather so it would do, if we possessed all the lines. Some
eleven lines appear to be missing, an inference that is
made in the following way. Taking the initial letters of
the surviving lines of the first oracle as an acrostic, we
get the following line, our missing first line

ΟΙΡΑΝ ΟΠΙΣΘΟΜΑ ΦΥ ΠΑΣ ΕΙΣ ΤΟΠΟΝ ΕΛΘ

which makes only partial sense. The conjectural addition of certain letters, eleven in all as indicated below,
possibly restores the original sense:

[Μ]ΟΙΡΑΝ ΟΠΙΣΘΟΜΑ[ΘΩΝ ΤΙΝ Ε]ΦΥ ΠΑΣ ΕΙΣ ΤΟΠΟΝ ΕΛΘ[ΕΙΝ]

If the scholarly restorations are correct, we possess twenty-nine of the original forty lines of the oracle.

On Phlegon's Sibylline oracles as acrostics see Diels 25–37, and on acrostics in Greek poetry generally see Ernst Vogt, 'Das Akrostichon in der griechischen Literatur,' *Antike und Abendland* 13 (1967) 80–95.

1–2 **all the prodigies.** The Sibyl foresees all the prodigies that will occur in the future, including that of the present hermaphrodite, whose birth she presently predicts (vv. 3–5) and the remedies for which she then focuses upon.

2 **This loom of mine.** That is, the loom of fate = prophecy.

3 **Trusting in its** (i.e., the loom's) **strength.** That the consultant must trust in the revelation is a recurrent theme in this and other literary oracles (e.g., Herodotos 1.66), as Diels (68 note 1) points out.

7 **Sacrifices for Demeter and holy Persephone.** The propitiation will be directed primarily towards chthonic deities, goddesses of death and fertility.

8 **By means of my loom, etc.** The text of the line is uncertain; see Morel 174–75.

sovereign goddess that I am. The Sibyl apparently identifies herself with Moira 'fate' (Diels 117).

[sacrifices that you should perform]. I enclose in brackets words that may be conjecturally supplied in order for the utterances to make clearer sense.

10ff. So far as the text is preserved, the Sibyl's *procuratio*, or remedy, is as follows:

1 Collect money to offer to Demeter (10–12)

2 Sacrifice 3 × 9 bulls (to Zeus? Demeter?) (13)

3 Maidens to sacrifice white cows to and make supplication according to Greek ritual in honour of the queen (Hera?) (13–18)

4 Matrons to offer thrice so many libations regularly (18–19)

5 Matrons to offer torches to Demeter (20–21)

6 Matrons to treble the libations (21–23)

7 Maidens to make same offering to Persephone and to make supplication (24–28)

8 Youths and maidens to offer money (29).

10 **a treasure of coin.** The different towns will make contributions of money (Latin *stips*) toward the expense of the sacrifice.

11 **from yourselves.** I retain the reading of the manuscript αὐτῶν (= ὑμῶν αὐτῶν) 'from yourselves' in preference to the emendation ἀστέων 'from towns' printed by Giannini in his text.

13 **Thrice nine bulls.** The Sibyl is fond of multiples of three, as Diels (40–43) observes. Three is a cultural number, or pattern number, among Greeks, Romans and other Indo-Europeans; see William Hansen, 'Three a Third Time', *Classical Journal* 71 (1976) 253–54.

Because of the loss of the following lines, we do not learn which deity is to be the recipient of the sacrifice of bulls. Diels supposes Zeus; Doria, Demeter (Doria 18–19).

14 When the text resumes, the speaker is now speaking of female sacrificial victims, perhaps cows, whereas before the lacuna the sacrificial animals were bulls.

16 **The same number of girls.** Probably twenty-seven (that is, 3 × 9), apparently the standard number in a chorus of girls for such rites; see Doria 19, 120–36.

17 **the deathless queen.** Perhaps Hera rather than Demeter, since the victims are white (in general, white victims were thought more appropriate for celestial deities, black for chthonic deities); for the Romans, Juno Regina.

20 **carry bright light.** The injunction is explained as being an allusion either to the ritual use of torches in nocturnal, expiatory rites (den Boer 107–08) or to the Greek custom of torch-races in honour of Demeter (Doria 21).

24 **Ploutonis.** Persephone, wife of Plouton (Latin *Pluto*), that is, Hades, lord of the dead.

26 **children.** The oracle carefully distinguishes females by age (old women, wives, maidens and children), assigning different roles to different age-groups.

28 **And for forgetfulness.** The text of this line is uncertain and disputed; see Doria 22–24.

Second Oracle

The content and acrostics of the lines that follow verse 29 in the manuscript indicate that they probably belong to a separate oracle (in the manuscript the verses appear as a single utterance). The gist of it is as follows:

1 Clothing to be offered to Persephone (30–31)
2 Persephone to be given the most beautiful thing in the world (32–34)
3 Black ox to be sacrificed to Hades; sacrificial procession of men in festive attire (37–40)
4 Disbelievers are not to participate (41–43)
5 Goat to be sacrificed to Apollo (44–47)
6 Prayer to made to Apollo with garlanded head (48–49)
7 White cow to be sacrificed to Hera (50–51)

8 Hymn to be sung (probably by the maidens) (52)
9 Allusion to settlement of Cumae and establishment of cult of Hera (53–56)
10 Libations and other daily offerings to Hera (58–60)
11 Sheep to be sacrificed to the chthonic deities (62)
12 Help will come for you (63–69)
13 Transitional lines (70–71).

The oracle gives detailed instructions for the expiation of a number of deities, with continued offerings to hold off a recurrence; however, the disaster can only be postponed, not averted, and will come in the distant future.

Because of the acrostics we know what the initial line should be, but inasmuch as the first line does not in fact correspond to the acrostics, it must not represent the actual beginning of the poem. The reason seems not to be that the line is counterfeit but that the poem in its full state is too long for a single initial line to answer to all the vertical acrostics. Diels points out that the Sibylline acrostic system permits a poem of up to fifty verses, since the maximum number of letters that can be found in a single hexametric line is fifty. What if the message should require more lines? Then, Diels conjectures, the first *two* lines of the oracle would preview the acrostics to follow. The verse that can be restored here from the extant lines might then be the *second* line of the intact oracle, and the true first line and its corresponding acrostics are missing (Diels 28 ff.). There is more. The extant lines that apparently correspond to line 2 make up verses 30–66, but the oracle actually continues for four more lines, so that presumably there were at least three lead verses. Thus:

a missing first line

b ΙΠΠΩΙ ΑΓΑΛΛΟΜΕΝΟΣ ΠΑΛΙΝ ΑΥ [ΚΑ]ΚΟΝ ΕΙΣ ΝΕΟΝ ΗΞΕΙ = restored second line = 'Exulting in his horse he will return home again only to find new troubles'

c ΑΥΤΑ[Ρ] . . . = restored beginning of third line = 'But . . .'

a' *c.*36 missing lines, answering acrostically to the missing first line

b' lines 30–66, answering acrostically to the missing second line

c' lines 67–70, answering acrostically to the beginning of the missing third line.

30 The text begins in mid-sentence, perhaps with the familiar thought 'trusting in my loom' (= prophecy).

34 **gift mixed with the loom.** Evidently the beautiful gift, whatever it may be, is to be accompanied by an article of clothing (Diels 118; cf. Doria 27).

36 **the yoke.** Presumably used metaphorically for slavery or foreign domination.

37 **Aidoneus Plouton.** Hades.

45 **Phoibos.** That is, Phoibos Apollo = Apollo.

48 **Phoibos Paieon.** Apollo.

52 I follow Diels rather than Giannini in reading αἵ (relative pronoun) rather than αἱ (interrogative).

53–56 **When the inhabitants.** Sibyl foretells the origin of Cumae, a Euboean Greek colony founded on the west coast of Italy in the eighth century BC, and of the establishment therein of the cult of Hera. The Greeks occupied first the offshore islands and then the mainland site itself. The reference implies that the present utterances are older than Cumae, and that the prophetess is specifically the Sibyl of Cumae.

57 **[The evil] will come.** The Greek has a verb meaning 'will come,' but the verb has no explicit subject. Diels (119) supplies 'calamity' as the subject, the sense then being: 'If you perform the prescribed rites, the calamity will still come, but it will not come in your lifetime.'

Alternatively one could understand as subject 'Hera,' which seems less drastic than importing 'calamity,' but the resulting thought seems unlikely.

(60) Guided by the acrostics, editors have corrected the received sequence of two verses.

62 With this line the ritual instructions as such come to an end.

63 **temples of Hera.** Salvation in the present depends upon adhering to and extending the model of worship established by the original Cumaean settlers, who introduced the cult of Hera (den Boer 109–10).

65 **On my leaves.** A reference to the palm leaves upon which, according to one tradition, the Cumaean Sibyl writes her prophecies (Diels 56–57 note 4). So Servius (*ad Verg. Aen.* 3.444): *in foliis palmarum Sibyllam scribere solere testatur Varro.*

shuttle. Used metonymically for 'loom' (Diels 120), i.e., prophecy, prophesying.

66 **eyes.** Reading ὄσσ' ('eyes') with Diels rather than ὄσσ' ('as many as') with Giannini.

66–7 **leaves of the . . . olive-tree.** The Sibyl, speaking metonymically, means a branch or garland of olive. Diels (119–24) argues that her actions indicate that she adopts the trappings of a suppliant, taking on the guilt of the people and entreating the angry gods on their behalf for deliverance.

68 **other newborn creatures.** Other prodigies such as the present hermaphroditic child.

69 **a Trojan.** The enigmatic allusion to a Trojan liberator has most often been taken as a reference to Sulla (Doria 265–79), but Hadrian (den Boer 111) and the Roman people (MacBain 135) also have their champions.

and from the land of Greece. The sense of the clause (ἅμα δ' Ἑλλάδος ἐκ γῆς) is uncertain; indeed, Diels supposes that it bears the opposite sense: 'and from the land of Greece [help will come]'.

70 The Sibyl signals an end to the digression of verses 57–69 (Diels 124), and the text of the oracle breaks off in mid-thought.

Phlegon's entry concludes with the oracle, so that we learn nothing of the disposition of the hermaphrodite—to judge from the cases mentioned in Livy and Julius Obsequens, the *haruspices* ('diviners') would have drowned it in a box in a river—or of the action taken on the oracles, but it is safe to guess that the instructions were carried out, as Livy and Julius Obsequens report in many other instances.

Finds of Giant Bones

The subject of hermaphrodites leads to the incidence of other physical monstrosities, which Phlegon takes up in two groups. The first concerns the remains of grotesque or in most cases huge humanoid beings of the distant or indefinite past (Chapters 11–19). The wonder is the astonishingly great magnitude of beings in the past in comparison with the norm of the present day. The second groups deals with human oddities in recent times (Chapters 20–25).

It was a common notion among the Greeks that mortals of earlier times were of greater stature than the folk of the present day, and in this trait resembled the gods. Homer describes the god Ares, sprawled out upon the battlefield of Troy after Athena had struck him with a stone, as extending seven *pelethra* (*Iliad* 21.407), a measurement that in later times at least signified 100 feet long (or, as a measurement of area, a 100 foot square = 10,000 square feet), so that he is some 700 feet in length. The same poet says that the giant Tityos, a son of Gaia (Earth), lying on the ground in Hades' realm where birds nibble on his liver in punishment for his misdeeds in life, extends nine *pelethra* (*Odyssey* 11.577). Aristotle alludes to the general belief that, with respect to body and soul, the gods and the heroes greatly exceed mankind (*Pol.* 7.13.3 = 1,332b), and Pausanias, describing a statue of a particular athlete at Olympia, remarks: 'He was the largest of all human beings, except for the so-called heroes and for any race of mortals that may have preceded the heroes. But of human beings of the present time this man, Poulydamas, son of Nikias, is the largest' (6.5.1).

A similar spirit underlay the folk belief that prehistoric structures made of huge blocks of stone, such as the fortress at Mycenae, had been built by giant masons, specifically the Kyklopes (Cyclopes), for which reason the Greeks referred to these structures as 'Cyclopean' (e.g., Hellanikos *FGH* 4 F 88, Bacchylides 11.77–79, Euripides *Hercules* 15 and 944, Strabo 8.6.11). In the same way modern Greek peasants describe the ancient Greeks (οἱ παλιοὶ Ἕλληνες) themselves as being giants. The ancients built this or that structure without even the use of tools. Finds of large bones attest to their great size. See Ἰ. Θ. Κακριδής, Οἱ Ἀρχαῖοι Ἕλληνες στη Νεοελληνικὴ Λαϊκὴ Παράδοση, 2nd edn (Ἀθῆνα 1979) 17–27.

Antiquity shows the same articulation between the chance finds of bones revealed by earthquakes, storms, excavations and the like, and the common belief that earlier persons were larger than the humans of today. Herodotos recounts how the coffin and bones of a man seven cubits long were discovered in Tegea, identified by means of an oracle as belonging to the hero Orestes, and conveyed to Sparta (1.67–68). Kimon, also aided by an oracle, discovered on the island of Skyros the large bones of the hero Theseus together with some associated artifacts and brought them to Athens, where they were displayed in a shrine (Plutarch *Theseus* 35–36, *Kimon* 8.5–6; Diodoros Sikelos 4.62.4; Pausanias 1.17.6). The colossal bones of other giants, heroes, and less easily classifiable persons, both famous and obscure, are mentioned in other authors, most richly in the guidebook of the traveller Pausanias and in the *Heroikos* of Philostratos. Smaller relics were also treasured. Pelops' sizable shoulder blade was rediscovered and kept at Elis (Pausanias 5.13.4–6; Pliny *NH* 28.34), and the Skythians pointed out to visitors a footprint two cubits long that Herakles had made on a rock (Herodotos 4.82; cf. Herodotos 2.91.3). This sort of thing is parodied by Lucian, who relates that in the course of his exploring a distant and unknown island he came upon a footprint 100 feet long that had been left on a rock by Herakles (*Vera Historia* 1.7).

In short, the popular interpretation of bones and the like was common in the ancient world, and the generally accepted interpretation of large, humanoid bones was that they were the remains of earlier mortal inhabitants of the earth. Of course the Greeks and Romans were not unique in this respect, and examples of the unscientific interpretation of bones and other early remains from chance finds could easily be added from other nations and from all periods for which there are records. In general see Pfister (1912) 2: 425–28, 507–09; S. Eitrem, 'Zu Philostrats Heroikos', *Symbolae Osloenses* 8 (1929) 1–56, at 53–56; Adrienne Mayor, 'Griffins and Arimaspeans', *Folklore* 104 (1993) 40–66, at 48–49; and Garland 173.

11 Idas

1 **Apollonios.** The identity of Apollonios is uncertain, and the name is very common—some twenty-seven authors of this name are listed in Luci Berkowitz and Karl A. Squitier, *Canon of Greek Authors and Works*, 2nd edn, New York 1986, but he is likely to be Apollonios the grammarian (γραμματικός), whom Phlegon cites as his source for Chapter 13, below. And since Phlegon continues with the theme of giant bones, eventually introducing Chapter 17 with 'The same author says,' he may be drawing upon Apollonios more or less continuously from Chapters 11 to 17.

a storage jar . . . broke apart in a powerful storm.
Similarly, Pausanias (1.35.7) mentions a Lydian tradition according to which a storm opened up an old
grave on a hill, uncovering unusually large bones,
which the local experts said were those of Hyllos, son
of Ge (Earth).

2 **Idas.** The archer Idas figures sometimes alone and
sometimes with his brother Lynkeus in a number of
stories set in the Heroic Age. He contends with the god
Apollo over a maiden, joins in the hunt for the
Calydonian boar, sails with the Argonauts in search of
the Golden Fleece, and rustles cattle with the Dioscuri.
He is described as the strongest man of his time and
extremely brave (Homer *Iliad* 9.558–59, Apollonios
Rhodios *Argo.* 1.151). See Roscher 2: 96–103 and
Gantz 89–90, 181, 196 for the sources and content of
his legend.

I know of no obvious reason why Idas should have
the grotesque features of a triple head and two sets of
teeth, attributes that to my knowledge are not
mentioned elsewhere. Idas, however, is the type of the
strong man, and in oral narrative a quality frequently is
expressed as a quantity, multiple limbs being a common
way of conveying the idea of physical strength, as in the
case of Kottos, Briareos and Gyges, three monstrous
offspring of Gaia (Earth) and Ouranos (Sky) who each
possess fifty heads and a hundred arms and whose principal quality is their strength (Hesiod *Theogony*
147–53).

According to Pausanias, a grave of Idas and Lynkeus
was pointed out in Sparta. Pausanias himself thinks
that the brothers are more likely to have been buried in
Messenia, but because much information about
Messenian antiquities had been lost, the Messenians
themselves (he says) do not know anything about the
matter, with the result that others are able to dispute

where the two lie buried (3.13.1–2). The tradition reported by Phlegon does locate Idas's burial in his homeland of Messenia, and perhaps this is its main point. The Messenians rediscover that their hero of olden times is in fact interred in their land, where they resolve to take proper care of him.

Homer. *Iliad* 9.558–60. The allusion is to the fight of the mortal Idas and the god Apollo for Marpessa, who was either Idas's betrothed or a maiden he was carrying away to marry. In his exceeding strength and boldness, Idas was not afraid to draw his bow against Apollo. According to one version Zeus intervened and allowed Marpessa to choose between the two, and she, thinking that the god might leave her when she became old, chose the mortal Idas (e.g., Apollodoros *Bibl.* 1.7.8–9).

12 The Cave of Artemis

bodies. By 'bodies' Phlegon means 'skeletons' here and in Chapter 14.

eleven cubits. A cubit is approximately 18 inches, so that the size of the rib-bones is about sixteen feet.

13–14 A Giant Tooth

Although Chapters 13–14 are numbered separately by editors they form a continuous narrative.

Apollonios the grammarian. On Apollonios, see the comment on Chapter 11, above.

Tiberius Nero. The emperor Tiberius, who reigned AD 14–37.

1–2 the earthquake. The narrator represents seismic activity
in Asia Minor and in Sicily as aspects of a single earthquake.

Deeply buried bones are revealed by an earthquake
here and in Chapter 19. Pliny (*NH* 7.16.73) similarly
reports that when a mountain in Crete was ruptured by
an earthquake, a body was discovered that was forty-
six cubits in height (= *c*.sixty-nine feet), some persons
thinking that it was Orion, others that it was Otos (two
giants in Greek mythology); the Cretan giant is also
mentioned by Solinus (1.91), who gives its height as
thirty-three cubits, and Philodemos of Gadara (*De
Signis* 4 De Lacy), who lists it as forty-eight.

2 they sent to Rome. The presentation of an extraordinary find to a ruler often happened in reality and is a
commonplace in traditional story. Phlegon relates how
a hermaphrodite was presented to the Emperor
Claudius (Chapter 6), how a child with multiple body
parts was brought to the Emperor Nero (Chapter 20),
and how the body of a centaur captured in Arabia was
sent to the emperor in Rome (Chapters 34–35). The
practice, which could operate on a small as well as on
a large scale, was certainly an old one. A Samian fish-
erman who caught a particularly large and fine fish
presented it as a gift to Polykrates, the ruler of the
island (Herodotos 3.42). A friend of Porphyry had a
slave who understood the language of birds and so also
their prophecies of future events; in order that he *not* be
sent as a gift to the emperor, his mother urinated into
his ears while he slept, causing him to lose his gift
(Porphyry *De Abstinentia* 3.3.7). A Roman craftsman
who devised an unbreakable glass bottle brought his
invention to the emperor (Petronius *Sat.* 51). In sum, as
Galen says, to kings the finest things from all quarters
are conveyed (*De Antidotis* 1.4 Kühn vol. 14, p. 25).

a tooth . . . not just a foot long but even greater. Augustine also reports having seen, in the company of other persons, an enormous human molar on the shore of Utica, a city in Africa near Hippo, and supposes that it belonged to a giant. They judged that if the tooth should be cut into pieces the size of their own molars, it could make a hundred of them (*De Civitate Dei* 15.9).

3 **Tiberius devised a shrewd plan.** The emperor's cleverness, tactful aristocratic style, and piety are illustrated in his response. Unlike the common people, who must see the wonder itself in order to appreciate it, the monarch is satisfied with the mere idea of it; moreover, he handles the matter in such a way that he offends neither the delegation of his subjects nor the remains of the dead.

15 An Exhibit of Bones

1 **bodies are exhibited.** For the public display and the archival storage of wonders, see the comment on Chapter 35, below.

2 **near to gods.** This vague phrase presumably means that before the celestial gods withdrew from earth to Olympos, living things used to grow *in the nearness* of gods, flourishing because of the divine presence; or possibly that in earlier times living things used to grow *nearer* to the celestial gods, that is, *taller*.

running down . . . shrinking. Applied to fire the Greek verb μαραίνομαι means to 'go slowly out'; applied to a person suffering from illness, 'waste or wither away'; applied to a sound, 'die away'; applied to wind, 'abate'; and so on. Phlegon uses the word here both of the passage of time and of the magnitude of successive generations of living things.

the sizes of creatures have been shrinking. If the humans of today are not as large as the men of old, the idea is near at hand that successive generations of humans have been getting smaller. This was doubtless a wide-spread assumption in antiquity. According to Pliny, one can almost observe that the human race is becoming shorter in stature each day: for a son to exceed his father in height is a rarity. The reason for this (he says) is that the conflagration to which the age is headed is consuming the fertility of semen. Pliny goes on to cite evidence, such as the discovery of giant skeletons, for the greater height of persons in earlier times (*NH* 7.16.73). Augustine, relating Italian and Hebrew traditions, argues that humans have experienced a decline not only in stature and but also in longevity (*De Civitate Dei* 15.9).

Phlegon never offers an explanation for wonders— except here, where he relates a phenomenon to a supposed general process of nature, that of cosmic senescence. The idea is that, like a human being, the earth comes into being, enjoys an energetic and fertile youth, settles into a less productive middle age, becomes old, and eventually perishes, and that a cosmic sympathy exists between the earth and all other things, which therefore flourish early in the cycle and then decline with the earth as it naturally ages and winds down. Adherents of the notion of cosmic degeneration, depending upon how optimistically or pessimistically they assessed the state of things, identified the current stage as its childhood, its middle years, or its later years. Thus, Aulus Gellius wonders if it is true that the bodies of the ancients were taller and broader than the bodies of persons in his own day and that in a senescent world things and humans have shrunk (*Noctes Atticae* 3.10). The diminishing size of human beings, then, is part of the overall diminishing fertility and energy of

the universe. Human stature runs parallel to cosmic
time: both are withering away. In different forms these
ideas had a place in Greco-Roman mythology, philosophy and popular speculation; see Arthur O.
Lovejoy and George Boas, *Primitivism and Related Ideas in
Antiquity* (New York 1965/1935), 98–102, and W.K.C.
Guthrie, *In the Beginning: Some Greek Views on the
Origins of Life and the Early State of Man*, Ithaca
1957. For Persian and Indian analogues, including the
detail that the stature of humans shrinks in concert
with the degeneration of the universe, see West 174–76.

16 Rhodes

reports of bones . . . so huge. Phlegon's account is vague.

17 The Coffin of Makroseiris

The same author says. See the comment on Apollonios
in Chapter 11, above.

there was a certain island. The introduction seems to
exist mostly to contextualize the epigram, which identifies the deceased by name and opposes the diminutive
size of his final resting-place to the great length of his
life. But the introductory narrative also reveals that the
deceased was of astonishingly great physical stature—
the feature that has induced Phlegon to file the item
here—so that he combines great stature and great
longevity, traits that individually or together are often
associated with the first humans. Just as humans have
been diminishing in size, so also their lifespans have
been shrinking.

As they were digging. The chance discovery of huge
bones by persons excavating for construction is found
also in Chapter 18.

a hundred cubits long. About 150 feet.

I, Makroseiris. In ancient epitaphs the deceased is often represented as addressing the reader. A mention of name, place of burial and years lived, as here, are among the kinds of information commonly given in epitaphs that emphasize biography. See Richmond Lattimore, *Themes in Greek and Latin Epitaphs*, Urbana 1962, 266–75. The epitaph, consisting of two iambic trimeters, is odd only in the incredibly long lifespan that it claims. Altogether the story of the discovery of Makroseiris presents an ironic contrast between the evident insignificance of the small and nameless island and the presumable importance of a being who achieved amazing greatness in size and years.

Makroseiris. That is, 'Long-Osiris'. The compound is formed from the Greek adjective μακρός 'makros' and the Egyptian divine name Osiris. Unless the name is simply another way of saying Great Osiris, it seems to reflect its bearer's great size and age, since the adjective *makros* can be used of height ('tall') and time ('long').

The presence in this narrative of a coffin and an Osiris vaguely recalls these elements in the Egyptian myth of Osiris, as it is reported by the Greek essayist Plutarch shortly before the time of Phlegon, for a coffin, or at least a chest, is a prominent feature of the story. His enemy Typhon (that is, the Egyptian god Seth) had a beautiful chest constructed corresponding to Osiris's height, and at a feast playfully offered to present it to the person who matched it in length. When Osiris lay down in the chest to try it out, Typhon and his fellow conspirators slammed down the lid, sealed it with lead, and put the chest in the river, from where it made its way to the sea. Osiris's sister Isis retrieved the coffin containing her dead brother, and later Typhon came upon it (*de Iside et Osiride* 14–18, *Mor.* 356d–58b). But in other respects Phlegon's narrative and the Egyptian myth do not congrue at all. Osiris did not remain interred in one coffin and certainly not on a Greek island; instead, pieces of him were buried at different sites all over Egypt. Moreover, he lived only a short while, for according to Plutarch either his life or his reign amounted to no more than twenty-eight years (42, *Mor.* 368a).

18 Carthage

Eumachos. Eumachos (*FGH* 178 F 2) was a Neapolitan historian of the third and second centuries BC whose work is lost except for a couple citations.

twenty-four cubits. About thirty-five feet.

19 Bosporos

1 Theopompos of Sinope. An otherwise unknown author. Sinope is situated on the southern coast of the Euxine Sea; the narrative that follows transpires at the northern end of the same sea.

twenty-four cubits. The skeleton matches the Carthaginian giants (Chapter 18) in its dimension but is less than a quarter the size of Makroseiris (Chapter 17). To put the matter into perspective, the tallest person whose height has been reliably documented in modern times is an adult male who in 1940, the year of his death, measured 8 feet, 11.1 inches (Young 6–7). There seems to have been a tradition that the usual height of heroes was about ten cubits, or fifteen feet (τὰ λεγόμενα δὲ περὶ τοῦ μεγέθους τῶν ἡρώων, ὡς δεκαπήχεις ἦσαν: Philostratos *Heroikos* 136), but in fact the sizes reported for different finds vary wildly; see S. Eitrem's excursus, 'Die Größe der Heroen', in *Symbolae Osloenses* 8 (1929) 53–56. If successive generations of human beings have been diminishing in height (Chapter 15), one should of course expect to find persons of different size, representing successive generations of smaller stature; however, no ancient author seems to make this argument, and certainly not Phlegon, who shows little interest in explanations of any sort.

2 **the local barbarian inhabitants cast the bones into the Maiotis Sea.** The implication is that, unlike civilized folk, who exhibit wonders in museums (Chapter 15) or send them to emperors and kings (Chapters 13–14), barbarians stupidly discard them, so that they cannot be studied or verified or serve as objects of curiosity.

Monstrous Births

The gigantic size of earlier populations leads to a collection of reports of physiologically abnormal births in recent times (Chapters 20–25); hermaphrodites might have been included here but are not, because they have already been treated. Phlegon arranges the entries chronologically, which results in the separation of some items that are thematically related.

The usual term for strikingly abnormal offspring in Greek is τέρας (*teras*, genitive *teratos*), from which the modern term 'teratology' derives, the study of congenital malformations; in Latin, *monstrum* and *prodigium* are common terms. Since these same words can signify a divine omen portending evil, it is obvious that children with manifest congenital abnormalities were, or could be, understood as portents sent by angry gods, signs of misfortune to come if the community should not set things aright. Although this interpretation of human oddities was common in antiquity, it was not confined to ancient times, for not until the early nineteenth century was it was established scientifically that human malformations were not the result of supernatural agency. For Aristotle's teratological work see Garland, for early modern researches see Park and Daston, and for a brief history of the subject from the viewpoints of folk belief and of medical science, see Pilgrim 5–17.

One may wonder why the huge inhabitants of the early earth should not have been regarded as prodigies as well, not to mention the satyrs and centaurs with their mixtures of human and animal parts. The explanation, at least in part, seems to lie in the ancient conception of a *teras* as a creature that is unlike its parents (Aeschines *Against Ktesiphon* 111, Aristotle *GA* 4.3.767b); consequently, among the divine blessings of a just community is that the women bear children like their parents (Hesiod *Works and Days* 235). See Delcourt 1938: 10–13; West 215–16. In this sense the mortals that preceded today's human beings were not *terata* because in all essentials they were like their parents, who also were large in stature, whereas hermaphrodites can be classified as *terata* because they are anomalies with respect to the species from which they spring: there never has been a self-reproducing community of hermaphrodites. Similarly, the ancients seem to have imagined satyrs and centaurs vaguely as special species of beings, unlike, say, the Minotaur, which was a unique monstrosity.

Probably Empedokles had in mind human oddities *inter alia* when he declared that in the stage of the cosmic cycle in which Eros (Love), as opposed to Eris (Strife), was ascendant, isolated parts of humans and animals came into being—heads, arms, eyes and so on—and, responding to the force of Eros, joined with one another in chance combinations, so that one cluster might consist of two upper bodies and two heads, another might be a mixture of a human part and an ox part, and still another might combine male and female features. Combinations that did not work well together, such as a human head and the stomach of an ox, perished by natural selection, whereas well-functioning combinations persisted and became the creatures of today (Empedokles fr. 57–61 D–K; cf. Lucretius 5.837–54). In other words, the beings that were produced included some with too many or too few body parts, some incorporating both human and animal parts, and some hermaphrodites. Once the rule, they are now the exception. See Garland 174–76.

Many infants with manifest abnormalities were exposed in the wilderness or done away with in some other fashion, sometimes after having undergone public inspection by officials or professional interpretation by specialists in sacred matters; indeed, in some instances Greek and Roman law or custom required that abnormal offspring be exposed or drowned. At Sparta malformed infants were left in a place full of pits alongside Taügetos called the Apothetai, or Deposits (Plutarch *Lykourgos* 16.1–2). And yet not all infants met this fate. Plutarch, writing in the first and second centuries AD, chides persons at Rome who disregard the paintings, statues and even the attractive boys and women who were for sale, and instead frequent the Monstrosities Market (τὴν τῶν τεράτων ἀγοράν), looking for persons without calves, with short arms, with three eyes, with ostrich heads, and in general for creatures of mixed form and for other oddities. Such sights (he says) soon bring satiety and nausea, and persons who are curious about life's failures and the perversities to be found in the households of others should remind themselves that previous viewings of such beings have brought them no delight or other benefit (*de curiositate* 10, *Mor.* 520c). Whether the Monstrosities Market was an actual market-place for the buying and selling of human curiosities or a place for viewing them for a fee is not clear, but its existence indicates that some infants with markedly abnormal bodies were reared. On the disposition of deformed infants in antiquity see Delcourt 1938: 36–66, den Boer 98–150, Garland 13–18, and on the lives of malformed persons in antiquity see Garland 28–58. On the commercial exhibition of human oddities, especially in recent times, see Robert Bogdan, *Freak Show: Presenting Human Oddities for Amusement and Profit*, Chicago 1988.

20 Multiple Features

four heads . . . and a proportionate number of limbs. Chapters 20, 21, and 25 concern children born with multiple body parts. The first child (Chapter 20) is represented as having four heads, eight arms, and eight legs; that is, as being four children melded into one body. The second (Chapter 21) and third (Chapter 25) child each have an additional head growing from their body.

Persons, mostly infants, possessing a greater or smaller than usual inventory of external body parts appear very frequently in the list of prodigies compiled by Julius Obsequens (*Liber Prodigiorum* 12, 14, 20, 25, 26, 27a, 40, 50, 51, 52, 53); he catalogues physiologically abnormal animals in exactly the same way: a mule with three feet (15), a foal with five feet (24), etc. This sort of abnormality is amply attested in humans in modern times; see e.g. Frederick Drimmer, *Very Special People: The Struggle, Loves and Triumphs of Human Oddities*, New York 1976. Aristotle explained a redundancy of body parts as the result of the fusion of sperms; see Garland 155–56.

the consuls in Rome. From the names of the consuls the event in Chapter 20 can be dated to AD 61.

21 Multiple Features

This report probably belongs closely with the foregoing, as in the case of Chapter 15 and 16, above.

22 Animal Child

Chapters 22–4 have to do with a human woman's giving birth to an animal or to a child who is partly human and partly bestial.

when. The date of this event is AD 49.

monkey. It is of course tempting to rationalize a report such as this by assuming that the woman probably gave birth to a human child with simian features rather than to an actual monkey, after which oral storytelling exaggerated the marvel by transforming simile to metaphor: the infant who only looked like a monkey gradually became, in popular accounts, a monkey. And indeed microcephalic infants are said to show a resemblance to monkeys, which has perhaps inspired the folk belief that an expectant mother should not look upon monkeys, lest the prenatal impression influence her fetus (Pilgrim 7, Garland 151). The idea that women who have seen monkeys during sexual intercourse have given birth to children resembling monkeys is found in the learned medical-writer Soranos (*Gyn.* 1.39), a contemporary of Phlegon. Whether the present report arose in this way or not, palaephatistic interpretation of this sort becomes strained when it is applied to more extreme accounts, such as Pliny's report that a certain Greek woman, Alkippe, gave birth to an elephant (*NH* 7.3.34).

Oddly, in Greek fiction and oral story we find more frequent allusion to the reverse of this wonder or at least to the supposition of it, that occasionally animals may give birth to human beings. For example, in the *Aesop Romance* a farmer, informed by his overseer that a prodigy had occurred, asked whether a tree had borne fruit out of season or an animal had given birth to a quadruped with human features (*Vita Aesopi* G:10). The novelist Longos describes how a simple countrywoman, whose husband had come upon an exposed child being suckled by a goat, was amazed that goats might produce human children (*Daphnis and Chloe* 1.3).

23 Partly Animal Child

a child having the head of Anubis. The Egyptian deity
Anubis had the appearance of a jackal or of a jackal-
like dog, and was represented as a recumbent animal
or as an upright mixed-being with anthropomorphic
body and theriomorphic head; see George Hart,
A Dictionary of Egyptian Gods and Goddesses,
London and New York 1987, 21–26. Rather than
simply saying that the child had the head of a dog,
Phlegon compares it to Anubis either because the
overall image of the child's human body and canine
head was most familiar as that of the mixed-form
god Anubis, or because the child's head resembled
that of Anubis specifically in being jackal-like.
Moreover, he may have wished to avoid the word
'dog-headed' (κυνοκέφαλος), which was somewhat
imprecise, since it might mean a member of the exotic
species of partly human and partly canine folk, the Dog
Heads, who were said to dwell in Libya or India; and
the word had also developed the meaning 'baboon'. In
any case it is unlikely that Phlegon himself understands
the child's head as being only dog-*like*, a phenomenon
that in the context of his other wonders would not be
very remarkable, even if Greeks did often employ
animal imagery figuratively of human features, as in
Plutarch's mention of certain persons displayed in the
Monstrosities Market as being 'weasel-armed'
(γαλεάγκωνας), that is, 'short-armed', and 'ostrich-
headed' (στρουθοκεφάλους), probably signifying
'microcephalic' or, colloquially, 'pinheads'. Animal
imagery in the description of human oddities is
common in all periods of which we have record, as can
be illustrated in this English account of a much-
discussed child born in Krakow in 1543:

. . . although he were begotten of honorable parents, yet was he most horrible, deformed and fearefull, hauing eyes of the colour of fire, his mouth and nose like to the snoute of an Oxe, wyth an horne annexed thereunto like the trumpe of an Elephant, all hys backe shagge hairde like a dogge, and in place where other men be accustomed to have brests, he had two heads of an Ape, having above his nauell marked the eies of a cat, and ioyned to his knee and armes foure heades of a dog, with a grenning and fierce countenance: the palmes of his feet and handes were like to those of an ape: and amongst the rest, he had a taile turning vp so hie, that the height thereof was half an elle: who after he had liued foure houres died, saying only: 'Watch, the Lorde commeth' (E. Fenton, *Certaine Secrete wonders of Nature*, London 1569, cited by Ferguson 1: Part 4, p. 9).

Aristotle takes up this point in his *Generation of Animals*. People say (he declares) that a certain deformed person has the head of a ram, a calf has a human head, or a sheep has the head of an ox, but in fact such properties are only resemblances, as when someone jokingly compares an ugly person to this or that animal, and never actually occur in reality. For different creatures have gestation periods of dissimilar lengths, so that it is impossible for such creatures to mate with each other and produce mixed offspring, and it is similarly impossible for a mixed creature to form otherwise, because each creature can develop only in accordance with the gestation period that is proper to it (4.769b.13–25). People may describe deformed beings metaphorically in terms of other kinds of being, and they may intend their words literally, but the descriptions must be understood as similes, since it is physiologically impossible for truly mixed creatures to be generated.

the consuls in Rome. The date of the event is AD 65.

24 Animal Children

Tridentum. That is, modern Trento.

snakes . . . curled up into a ball. Snakes are the most commonly reported bestial offspring of humans. Pliny (*NH* 7.3.34) says that a maidservant once gave birth to a snake, which, because the event took place at the beginning of the Marsian, or Social, War (91–88 BC), was understood to be a portent; cf. also Appian *Civ.* 1.83. According to Julius Obsequens a married woman gave birth to a live snake in Clusium, Etruria, a few years later (83 BC); upon the instruction of the seers it was thrown into flowing water, and swam upstream (*Liber Prodigiorum* 57).

the consuls in Rome. The date is AD 83.

25 Multiple Features

baby . . . was cast into the Tiber River. Of the six cases of malformed or bestial offspring collected in this section, only in this one is the disposition mentioned. The events follow the scenario that is commonly attested in cases of hermaphroditic infants: discovery of physiologically abnormal child, consultation of interpreters of the sacred, destruction of child by burning or drowning (cf. Chapter 2, above). Similarly Julius Obsequens (*Liber Prodigiorum* 25) records that in the year 136 BC a maidservant gave birth to a boy with four feet, hands, eyes, and ears, and with two sets of genitals; on the instruction of the seers he was burnt up, and his ashes were thrown into the sea.

Three explanations of the cause of human oddities have enjoyed a long popularity (Pilgrim 5–9). A particular malformation is (1) a portent, and so is of supernatural origin; or it is of natural origin, at least as causality is conceived by the believer, and is the result of (2) a maternal impression or fright, or of (3) hybridity. It is probably safe to infer that the two-headed child described by Phlegon in this chapter, like the malformed child mentioned by Julius Obsequens, was taken anciently to be an instance of the first category, an aberration caused by the gods for the purpose of expressing and communicating their displeasure to a human group; and it may be that most infants with too many or too few body parts were so classified, for nearly all the instances of human *monstra* included by Julius Obsequens in his *Book of Prodigies* are of this sort.

But beings that seemed to combine features of different species or the like, as the Anubis-headed infant in Chapter 23, lent themselves to explanation alternatively as products of maternal impression or as hybrids, and doubtless they were sometimes so interpreted, for both ideas were current in antiquity. The process of maternal impression, that an image seen by a woman at the time of conception or later impresses itself somehow, causing the fetus physically to resemble the image, is cited as a fact of nature by several ancient authors, including the philosopher Empedokles (fr. 31A 81.20–22 DK) and the medical writer Soranos (*Gyn.* 1.39), who speak of women looking upon paintings, statues or monkeys at the moment of conception and subsequently giving birth to children that physically resembled these sights; see Garland 151. Maternal impression plays an important part in Heliodoros's novel of the third or fourth century AD, *Ethiopian Story*, which relates how a certain black couple produced a white daughter because at the moment of conception the woman had chanced to glance at a painting featuring a white maiden; fearing that she would be open to an accusation of adultery, the mother exposed her child (*Aithiopika* 4.8). In a similar way in the latter half of the nineteenth century John Merrick, the so-called Elephant Man, attributed his own deformity to a combination of maternal impression and maternal fright, citing the fact that a circus elephant had knocked down his mother, frightening her, sometime before his birth.

Only one example of a mixed creature appears in Julius Obsequens's list (*Book of Prodigies* 14)—in the year 163 BC at Caere a pig was born with human hands and feet; although Livy mentions others, for example, the birth of a boy with an elephant head (27.11.5–6) and a pig with a human head (31.12.7). It is found frequently in mythological narrative as the cause of mixed features. Thus, the rustic god Hermes and the nymph Dryope produced a son, Pan, a *teras* in appearance (τερατωπὸν ἰδέσθαι) with his goat-feet and horns; his mother ran away and his nurse was afraid, but Hermes himself was delighted (*HH Pan* 32–47). This instance is less precise than other narratives, since Hermes, although he is a god of rustics, does not himself possess goatish features, and most often ancient authors simply represent one parent of a mixed creature as human and the other as animal. So the monstrous Minotaur, a creature with the body of a man and the head of a bull, was the offspring of a woman and a bull (Apollodoros *Bibl.* 3.1.4). This idea is treated jocularly in an Aesopic fable in which the ewes of a certain farmer were giving birth to lambs with human heads. Frightened by the prodigy (*monstro territus*) the man consulted soothsayers, who each suggested one thing or another, whereas Aesop perceptively advised him to find wives for his shepherds (Phaedrus 3.3); Plutarch tells the same story of Thales, one of the seven wise men of archaic Greece (*Septem*

Sapientium Convivium 149c–e). In the realm of ethnography Pliny (*NH* 7.2.30) says that according to the Greek historian Douris there are Indians who mate with wild animals, producing offspring that are half-human and half-animal. And the rationalistic Diodoros Sikelos explains Hippocentaurs 'Horse-Centaurs' as springing originally from mares who once consorted with a clan of humans called Centaurs (4.70.1). Other examples could be adduced. Since the idea of hybridity is well attested in myth, fable, pseudo-ethnography and rationalist speculation, it must have been operative on the level of folk belief as well. An example of how the notion might have been applied to specific cases can be found in the seventeenth-century records of the New Haven colony. After a pig was born with a single eye in the middle of its face, the blame presently fell upon George Spencer, a servant who had one good eye and one false eye. He was tried and executed for 'abominable filthiness' (Pilgrim 8). Similarly a girl who gave birth to a child having the head of a cat was publically burnt alive in seventeenth-century Denmark for wantonly having had sexual intercourse with a cat (Garland 190). Clearly the implications for the parent(s) are much more drastic in the case of presumed hybridity than in the case of presumed maternal impression. For the woman who gave birth to the child with the head of Anubis (Chapter 23), it would have been the difference between the presumption that she had had sexual intercourse with an animal (or in this case possibly with the god) and the presumption that at a vulnerable moment in her pregnancy she had been frightened by a dog or had glanced at an image of Anubis. I suggest that the idea of hybridity found relatively more frequent expression in traditional story, where the idea was enjoyable but harmless, whereas in real life the less-threatening notion of maternal impression was more commonly invoked as an explanation.

the consuls. The date is AD 112.

Births from Males

The theme of wondrous births begun in Chapters 20–25 with *monstra* continues with two other kinds of unusual childbirth. First, Phlegon gives two instances of parturition by men (Chapters 26–27), in which the wondrous element, in addition to the general topsy-turviness of a man playing the woman's part, is the presumed impossibility of a man bearing a child, since the role of parturition is assigned to women on the basis, not of social convention, but of biology. And, second, he records four cases of the bearing of a very large number of children at a single time or in successive pregnancies (Chapters 28–31), expressing the marvel of abnormally great magnitude.

26 A Homosexual

The doctor Dorotheos. The works of the Greco-Egyptian medical doctor, Dorotheos of Heliopolis, have not survived and are known only from citations in other authors. Since he lived sometime before the first century AD, the event belongs to the first century BC or earlier.

a homosexual male. The word Phlegon uses is *kinaidos* (κίναιδος), which implies, not so much that the man was homosexual in our sense of the term, but that for whatever reason the role he assumed in the sexual act was that of the penetrated, receiving the semen of his sexual partner, the penetrator; see John J. Winkler, *The Constraints of Desire: The Anthropology of Sex and Gender in Ancient Greece*, New York and London

1990, 45–54. What is unusual is that he somehow became pregnant thereby and bore a child.

preserved. The infant did not live or was not allowed to live. On the preservation and exhibition of wonders see Chapters 15, 19, and 34–35.

27 A Slave

a male slave. Although details are not given, they are likely to be similar to those in the preceding chapter.

consuls. The date is AD 56. As usual, Phlegon's arrangment within a thematic cluster is chronological.

The theme of male pregnancy appears in Greek mythology but less straightforwardly than here. There is a strong hint of it in the Succession Myth in which Kronos, after castrating his father Ouranos (Sky), swallows each of his own offspring as soon as his wife Rheia gives birth, whereafter his children remain intact inside him until he is forced to spew them up (Hesiod *Theogony* 161–210, 453–500). The transfer of infants from mother's womb to father's belly seems almost like shared pregnancy and parturition, the mother relaying them to the father, although to be sure Kronos's motive is fear of displacement rather than fatherly affection. However, male pregnancy as such appears clearly enough in the cognate Hittite myth, in which Kumarbi bites off the genitals of Anu (Sky) and swallows them, as a result of which he becomes pregnant with several gods, giving birth to them through various parts of his body. For the text see Harry A. Hoffner, Jr., *Hittite Myths*, Atlanta 1990, no. 14 (The Song of Kumarbi), 40–43. The idea of male pregnancy and parturition reappears in Greek myth in the births of Athena and of Dionysos, who emerge from different parts of Zeus's body. In the former, Zeus swallows his pregnant wife Metis and in time gives birth to Athena from his head (Hesiod *Theogony* 886–929); in the latter, Zeus takes the fetus from his dead lover Semele and places it into his own thigh, whence later it is born. For the sources of the Semele myth and their variations see Gantz 473–77.

In general the theme of male pregnancy and parturition, as found in Greek myth, differs significantly from that in later legend. In myth the sexual relations are heterosexual, and the male only continues the pregnancy that the mother has begun, whereas in legend the sexual relations are homosexual, and the male is the sole bearer of the child. Although both traditions reveal a Greek fascination with male parturition, as narratives they are essentially independent of each other. Phlegon does not cite any of the mythic narratives because he prefers wonders of recent times to events of the distant, mythological past and because in any case the myths do not illustrate unambiguous male pregnancy.

Amazing Multiple Births

Contrary to his usual practice, Phlegon does not present this group of wonders chronologically but instead begins with the two events from recent times, capping them with the two events from the prehistoric, or mythological, period. The result is two thematic clusters, since the historical narratives emphasize the mothers, not even mentioning the fathers, whereas the mythological narratives foreground both parents. But probably Phlegon regards them as belonging to two different topics, one concerning multiple deliveries and multiple births by fertile mothers, the other concerning very large numbers of children begotten by fecund parents.

Multiple births beyond a certain magnitude were regarded as prodigious, at least by the Romans; see Delcourt 1938: 103–05. So Julius Obsequens (*Liber Prodigiorum* 14) lists the birth of triplets in 163 BC as a prodigy, although Pliny, citing two famous sets of triplets in Roman historical tradition, the Horatii and the Curiatii, declares that a multiple delivery is regarded as portentous (*inter ostenta ducitur*) if it *exceeds* three—except in Egypt, where he says drinking the water of the Nile promotes human fertility. Thus he mentions a plebeian woman named Fausta who gave birth to two male and two female babies, which he says clearly portended the food shortage that followed. Having made this point, Pliny goes on to describe a number of unusually fertile mothers, namely, a Peloponnesian woman who gave birth to quintuplets on four occasions, an Egyptian woman who gave birth to seven children in one delivery, and Eutychis of Tralles who gave birth thirty times during her life; she ranked as one of several marvels whom Pompey the Great celebrated in images in his theatre (*NH* 7.3.33–34). With regard to the last, one might have expected Phlegon to include his fellow Trallean among the other fecund women in the present section. Egypt is not the only place that promotes human fertility. According to the Greek paradoxographical compilation attributed to Aristotle (*Mirabilies Auscultationes* 80), Umbria is so fertile that animals produce offspring three times a year, plants bear very plentiful fruit, and most women give birth to twins or triplets. Although the author makes no evaluative comment, it appears that he regards these wonders as welcome rather than as portentous phenomena. And according to Dionysios of Halikarnassos the bearing of triplets was actually honored by the state because of the fine deed of the Horatii. The parents received from the public treasury monetary support for the rearing of the triplets until they were grown (3.22.10).

Despite these impressive statistics, the modern record for the most children born to one mother is even more astonishing, for according to our own book of wonders, *The Guinness Book of Records*, a woman in the course of twenty-seven confinements gave birth to sixty-nine children, including sixteen pairs of twins, seven triplets, and four quadruplets (Young 9).

28 An Alexandrian Woman

> **Antigonos.** Phlegon borrows this brief entry nearly word for word from the compilation of wonders made by Antigonos (*Mirabilia* 110.1), a paradoxographer of the third century BC.
>
> **four deliveries.** That is, four pregnancies.

29 Another Alexandrian Woman

> **1 Another woman from the same city.** This woman seems to have made quite an impression on Romans. In the codification of Roman laws known as the *Digest of Justinian*, the subject of multiple births arises on several occasions, and on each occasion the contributor is reminded of Serapias, whether he names her or not. Broaching the subject of 'incredible' multiple births, Paulus writes: 'It is reported that four girls have been born from a matron at a single time, and weighty authorities have reported that a woman from the Peloponnese gave birth to quadruplets on five occasions and that many women in Egypt have born septuplets. We have moreover seen triplets in the garb of senators—the Horatii. *Furthermore, Laelius writes that on the Palatium he saw a free woman who had been brought from Alexandria to be shown to Hadrian along with her five children, four of whom she had delivered at one time and the fifth forty days later'* (*Digesta* 5.4.3). Elsewhere Gaius mentions her, saying that she bore her quintuplets at the same time; like Pliny he is uncomfortable about multiple births above the number of three: 'In our own time Serapias, an

Alexandrian woman, was brought to the divine
Hadrian with her five children, whom she had delivered
at a single time. When however more than three
children are born, it seems almost monstrous
(*portentosum*)' (*Dig.* 34.5.7). Similarly, Julianus,
speaking of the possibility of multiple births up to the
number of five, writes: 'Even Aristotle wrote that five
children can be born, because a woman's womb has
that many receptacles. There was at Rome an
Alexandrian woman from Egypt who delivered five at
the same time, all of whom survived; this was
confirmed for me in Egypt' (*Dig.* 46.3.36). Julianus's
reference is to Aristotle's *History of Animals*, where the
philosopher says that the greatest number of children
that can be born at one time is five, that there have been
many confirmed instances of quintuplets, and that one
woman gave birth to twenty children in the course of
four births, bearing five each time (7.4.30). That
Serapias is probably the same woman as Phlegon's
unnamed Alexandrian mother of quintuplets is
suggested by Ludwig Friedländer, 'Exhibition of
Natural Curiosities at Rome', in *Roman Life and
Manners Under the Early Empire*, trans. A.B. Gough,
London and New York 1913, 4: 9.

the Emperor Trajan. Trajan reigned AD 98–117, which
signals the approximate dramatic date of the event. It is
unclear whether Trajan orders the children reared at his
expense because they include male triplets or because of
their total number.

30 Aigyptos

Hippostratos. A historian perhaps of the third century
BC, known only in citation; see (*FGH* 568 F 1).

Aigyptos. Like his brother Danaos in the following

chapter, Aigyptos figures in the legends of the heroic age, and the information about the two of them, which Phlegon's editors have divided into two entries, really belongs to a single, interlocked story. The gist of it is that Aigyptos begot fifty sons, and Danaos begot fifty daughters. The sons of Aigyptos pressed their cousins into marrying them, which they did, but all but one of the Danaids killed their husbands on their wedding night. After their own deaths the forty-nine murderesses carried on an existence of sorts in Hades' realm, transporting water in cracked pitchers or the like. For the legend see Roscher 1: 155–57, 949–54, 1,409 (7), 1430; Gantz 203–08.

The chapters on Aigyptos and Danaos are among the few mythological narratives included by Phlegon, the others being those of Teiresias and Kainis (Chapters 4–5). Like other paradoxographers Phlegon generally shows less interest in wonders from the remote past than in marvels of the recent past and of his own day.

fifty sons. No details are given about the number of pregnancies and the numbers of children born on individual occasions, since here Phlegon's interest lies more in the total number of children produced by a single couple.

The Greek mythological tradition features other productive parents. Mnemosyne bore the nine Muses after sleeping with Zeus for nine successive nights (Hesiod *Theogony* 53–67), a record for multiple births. Large families are found especially among sea deities: Hesiod names the fifty daughters whom Doris bears to her mate Nereus, and the twenty-five sons and forty-one daughters whom Tethys bears to her mate Okeanos, and he declares that all told Okeanos and Tethys have 3,000 daughters and as many sons (Hesiod *Theogony* 240–64, 337–70); however, none of these traditions really emphasizes parental productivity as a theme. The only mythological story that actually foregrounds human fertility as a significant issue is that of the proud Niobe, mother of some fourteen sons and daughters. When she boastfully compared herself and her many offspring to the goddess Leto with her mere two, Leto's children Apollo and Artemis slaughtered Niobe's fourteen (e.g., Apollodoros *Bibl.* 3.5.6).

one wife Euryrrhoe. According to the usual tradition, the brothers Aigyptos and Danaos fathered their hundred children not on one but on many wives (e.g., Apollodoros *Bibl.* 2.1.4–5). The less common version given by Phlegon, according to which each man had but a single wife, was known also to the Byzantine poet Tzetzes (*Chiliades* 7.364–71), and the tradition can be traced back to a single author, the historian Hippostratos (*FGH* 568 F 1), whom both authors cite.

31 Danaos

Europe, daughter of Neilos. Just as the husbands are brothers, so also the wives are sisters, both being daughters of the Nile River.

Abnormally Rapid Development

After dwelling on different aspects of birth (Chapters 20–31), Phlegon proceeds chronologically through the life-cycle, first giving two cases of abnormally rapid development (Chapters 32–33) and then concluding his book with death and corpses (Chapters 34–35). At this point he has come full circle, for logically his final chapters could lead into the theme with which his collection, at least in its present form, begins: the return of the dead to life.

The source of wonder in this section is great physiological velocity, a rapid rate of development in the human body in comparison with the norm, as though the person were racing through life (or as though he or she experienced time more slowly than others do). The opposite marvel would be the *makrobioi*, exceptionally long-lived persons, whose life proceeds with abnormal slowness relative to the rest of mankind, a wonder that Phlegon deals with not here but in his essay *Long-Lived Persons*.

32 An Unnamed Male

Krateros. The historian Krateros the Macedonian lived in the 4th and 3rd centuries BC; see *FGH* (342 T 4).

in the space of seven years. Other examples of individual persons who have sped developmentally through life are mentioned by Pliny, who observes that it is a well-known fact that some persons complete their *cursus vitae* by the age of three years. He cites the son of a certain Euthymenes, a Greek of Salamis, who grew to be three cubits tall (= four-and-a-half feet). The lad, who walked sluggishly and was mentally dull, went through puberty and acquired a deep voice before dying suddenly at the age of three. Pliny adds that he himself recently saw a male with all these traits except for the attainment of puberty. The Greeks, he explains, call such persons ἐκτράπελοι (*NH* 7.16.75–76); that is, 'deviants,' but connotatively 'monstrosities.'

The most apposite mythological analogue is Hesiod's fifth age of men, the race of iron, the final stage in Hesiod's account of cosmic degeneration. A signal of the final days of this age will be when babies are born with grey hair on their temples (*Works and Days* 181). At that time, then, human beings will pass swiftly through a brief life that skips all youth and middle age and proceeds immediately to senescence.

33 Women in Pandaia

Megasthenes. Phlegon credits as his source Megasthenes (*FGH* 715 F 13), a Greek historian and ethnographer of the fourth and third centuries BC, who had visited India and whose pioneering and uncritical book on the place has survived only in citations found in later authors.

the women who dwell in Pandaia. This wonder differs from the preceeding in that the phenomenon operates on the level of the community, for which it is the norm, however unusual it is for mankind in general, whereas in the previous instance (Chapter 32) the person constitutes an individual aberration, atypical both of his community and of mankind.

Not surprisingly the exceptional person belongs to the familiar world, whereas the abnormal community is located in an exotic land, for a single local marvel carries the same weight in wonder as a distant mass marvel, and a wondrous individual residing in an exotic land is scarcely worth reporting. In the same way monstrosities are reported locally on an individual level (Chapters 20–25) but in distant lands on the level of entire tribes and nations: different peoples of India are characterized as having their feet turned backward, as having eight toes on each foot, as having the heads of dogs, as having only one leg, as lacking necks, etc. (e.g., Pliny *NH* 7.2.22–23), all of these features being abnormalities that have been reported at one time or another of local human oddities. What is true of space is true also of time: wonders of the remote past, being easy to come by, are not worth as much, for which reason, I suggest, Phlegon and the other paradoxographers are less interested in the wondrous motifs of the mythological tradition than in those of their own day.

In my rendering I retain the 'Pandaia' of the manuscript rather than adopt Giannini's emendation of 'Padaia,' for which he compares the Indian tribe 'Padaioi' mentioned by Herodotos (3.99). Arrian (see below) knows the city as 'Pandaia,' and Pliny mentions the *gens Pandae* as the only kingdom in India that is ruled by women (*NH* 6.23.76), so that the emendation seems unjustified.

six years old. Although Phlegon does not explicitly identify the early age of child-bearing among the women of Pandaia as a feature of a rapid life-cycle, its placement in this section of his collection implies that quick and brief development is the underlying idea, and this was in fact Megasthenes's thought. According to Arrian, who draws in considerable detail upon the lost work of Megasthenes, a certain Herakles (whether the Greek hero or another is left uncertain) settled in India, where he begot many sons and one daughter, who was born to him late in life. He gave the region in which his daughter was born into her hands to rule over, naming it Pandaia after her. In this region the women are ripe for marriage at seven years of age and the men live no longer than forty years; and indeed when Herakles saw that his own end was near and that there was no man worthy of his daughter's hand, he wed his seven-year-old daughter himself, and from their union have sprung the rulers of Pandaia. Arrian also mentions, on the authority of Megasthenes, that fruits and vegetables in this region ripen more quickly than in other regions and also degenerate more quickly (Arrian *Indika* 8.4–9.8 = *FGH* 715 F 13). In short, both humans and fruits proceed through their natural cycles far more quickly in Pandaia than they do in the Mediterranean world.

Drawing upon the same Megasthenes, Pliny (*NH* 7.2.30) mentions that among a people of India called the Mandi, the women bear children at the age of seven years and are old at the age of forty; however, 'Mandi' is probably just an error for 'Pandi,' that is, the people of Pandaia, in which case this notice is really another version of Megasthenes' Pandaia. Pliny adds, on the authority of Douris of Samos (*FGH* 76 F 48), a sensationalistic Greek historian and a contemporary of Megasthenes, that among the Calingi, another people of India, the women conceive at the age of five years and do not live past their eighth year.

Megasthenes and Douris, then, describe exotic peoples of India who supposedly cycle through life very quickly, the Pandaioi/Mandi at around double-speed, since the women bear children at the age of seven, whereas for Greek and Roman females the usual age of menarche and marriage appears to have been about fourteen; see Darrel Amundsen and Carol Diers, 'The Age of Menarche in Classical Greece and Rome', *Human Biology* 41 (1969) 125–32. There was a tradition, then, among the Greeks of rapid cycles of development on the level of whole communities in parts of India. Presumably the same fertility that fostered life-forms of wondrous size and variety also promoted marvellously fast life-cycles.

Live Centaurs Discovered

34 A Hippocentaur

1 **hippocentaur.** That is, 'horse-centaur', a fabulous creature that is partly human (head, arms and upper body) and partly equine (trunk and four legs), also called simply 'centaur', but 'hippocentaur' is more precise, distinguishing the creature on the one hand from the Centaurs (Κένταυροι), a legendary people of Thessaly,

and on the other hand from the fabulous 'onocentaur' ('ass-centaur'; see Roscher 2: 1,068).

Saune. The identity of both the Arabian city and the poisonous drug of the same name appear to be unknown. Nor is it clear what relevance the drug has to the narrative of the centaur. Perhaps it is a gratuitous *paradoxon* (for another mysterious and deadly mountainous drug see e.g. pseudo-Aristotle *Mirabilies Auscultationes* 78), or perhaps the high mountain full of poisonous plants is intended to suggest just how difficult of access the habitat of the hippocentaurs is. The loftiness, at least, of their mountain with its thin air does prove to be significant, since the captured beast does not long survive the change of atmosphere.

2 **captured alive.** Pliny saw this very beast (*NH* 7.3.35). It had been preserved in honey and brought from Egypt to Rome during the reign of Claudius.

Ancient authors report the occasional capture of fabulous beings, and their corpses were often put on public display. At this distance, of course, it is impossible to determine which of these exhibits were instances of erroneous identification and which were deliberate frauds, although in their time they seem for the most part to have been accepted as genuine. An exception was a phoenix that reportedly had flown into Egypt and in AD 47 was brought to Rome. Exhibited in the Comitium it seems to have been regarded as a fake by everyone (Pliny *NH* 10.2.5; Tacitus *Annals* 6.28; cf. Dio 58.27.1); on its significance see Pighi 17–18.

The capture of a live satyr in 83 BC is described by Plutarch. When Sulla and his army were in Dyrrhachion, Greece, preparing to sail to Brundisium, a sleeping satyr was captured in nearby Nymphaion, a sacred place. He looked just the way sculptors and painters represent such creatures. He was brought before Sulla, where many interpreters asked him who he was, but he only uttered something scarcely intelligible, a harsh sound that was somewhere between that of a horse and a goat. Sulla was astounded, and the men escorted the satyr away (*Sulla* 27). Of the subsequent fate of this creature we hear nothing. According to Jerome, another satyr, this one preserved in salt, was sent to Antioch in order that the Emperor Constantine might view him (*Vita S. Pauli Primi Eremitae* 8 = Migne *PL* 23:24).

Nor did Tritons and Nereids elude human inspection. The people of Olisipo (Lisbon) sent a delegation to the Emperor Tiberius to inform him that a Triton had been seen and heard playing on a shell in a certain cave. Moreover, Pliny had it on the word of members of the equestrian order that the citizens of Gades (Cadiz) had seen a merman (*marinum hominem*, presumably a Triton) in the Gulf of Gades; resembling a human being in every respect, he liked to climb aboard boats during the night and sit on their side, which caused the vessels to tip and even to sink if he did not depart. As for Nereids, one had been spotted along the shoreline by the people of Olisipo; she corresponded to the usual image of Nereids except that she was hairy, and when she was dying her mournful song was heard by coastal dwellers at a great distance. Furthermore the governor of Gaul wrote to the Emperor Augustus about the large number of dead Nereids who lay on the shore there; and dead Nereids were reported to have washed up upon other shores as well (Pliny *NH* 9.4.9–11).

The body of a Triton was on display in Greece, and the corpse of another Triton ranked among the wonders of Rome. Pausanias saw them both. The former was exhibited in Tanagra in Boeotia, where two accounts of the creature's demise were current. According to one, he had attacked the women of Tanagra while they were swimming in the sea, ritually bathing themselves in preparation for the secret rites of Dionysos. But they called out to Dionysos, who appeared and overcame the Triton. According to the other, which for Pausanias was the more persuasive, the Triton used to ambush and carry off cattle that had been driven down to the sea and also used to attack small boats. So one day the Tanagrans left a bucket of wine for him. Smelling it he came at once, drank it and fell asleep on the beach, whereupon a Tanagran chopped off his head with an axe, for which reason the exhibited corpse had no head. Since the Triton had been overcome in a state of drunkenness, the Tanagrans credited Dionysos with the kill. The Roman Triton was smaller. Pausanias describes the hair on their head as resembling that of frogs in colour and texture; the rest of their body had fine scales similar to the rough skin of a shark. They had gills beneath their ears, a human nose, a rather broad mouth and the teeth of a wild animal. Their eyes seemed to him to be greyish. They had hands and fingers, and their fingernails were like the surface of sea shells. Beneath their chest and stomach there was a dolphin-like tail instead of feet (Pausanias 9.20.4–21.1). See further James G. Frazer, *Pausanias's Description of Greece*, London 1913, 5:83–85.

Capturing a nature-spirit by mixing wine into the pool from which he is accustomed to drink, or by placing wine in a vessel alongside the pool, is a familiar trick in traditional story (Herodotos 8.138; Xenophon *Anabasis* 1.2.13; Theopompos *Philippika* 8 (FGH 115 F 75); Pausanias 1.4.5; Philostratos *Life of Apollonios of Tyana* 6.27; Ovid *Fasti* 3.291–326; Plutarch *Numa* 15.3–4; see Karl Meuli, *Odyssee und Argonautika*,

Basel 1921, 71–73. It works because such creatures, being inexperienced in human culture, lack judgement and so are easy prey, as when the feral man Enkidu is captured by means of the harlot Shamhat in the Mesopotamian *Epic of Gilgamesh* (Tablet 1). Pausanias mentions a wild man who had been captured in Libya and sent to Rome as a marvel (2.21.6–7), and a fictional account of the capture of wild humans appears in Ps.–Kallisthenes's *Alexander Romance* (2.33).

A certain Demostratos also saw the preserved Triton at Tanagra, giving an account of it that Aelian draws upon in his book on animals. Demostratos said that the Triton looked like the portrayals of Tritons in statues and paintings except that his head had so degenerated in the course of time that it was difficult to discern much of it. Demostratos touched it, and hard scales fell off. An unnamed official who was not a Tanagran, wanting to test the nature of the creature's skin, removed a small piece and placed it in the fire. When it burnt a strong smell assailed the noses of the bystanders, although it remained unclear to them whether the animal was essentially terrestrial or marine. Demostratos added that the official paid dearly for his experiment, for shortly afterwards the man drowned in a boating accident. The Tanagrans attributed his misfortune to the fact that he had profaned the Triton, pointing out that when the man's lifeless corpse was brought ashore, it disgorged a fluid that smelled like the stench of the Triton's burning skin (Aelian *Historia Animalium* 13.21).

35 More Hippocentaurs

other hippocentaurs. Pliny mentions in passing that communities of satyrs, among other even more fantastic beings and peoples, were found in Africa and

India (*NH* 5.8.44–46, 7.2.24); for the history of this idea see Wittkower 191.

the emperor's storehouse. If the emperor's subjects were pleased to present him with material curiosities, he would presently have a store of marvels, and indeed Augustus is said to have possessed a personal collection of precisely such things: the remains of huge sea-monsters and other animals, bones of the race of Giants, and weapons that had belonged to the heroes of old (Suetonius *Divus Augustus* 72). For the emperors as patrons of living human oddities see Garland 48–50.

In addition to private collections, many such wonders were on more or less permanent public exhibition (see Chapters 15, 19, 26), especially in temples and their grounds, which often were museums in all but name, and in later times in churches. In the Temple of Athena in Tegea, for example, you could see such mythological wonders as the skin and tusks of the Calydonian Boar—or at least you could until Augustus made off with the tusks (Pausanias 8.46.1 and 47.2), and in the sanctuary of Hilaeira and Phoibe in Sparta you could examine the very egg that Leda laid, which was hanging by ribbons from the ceiling (Pausanias 3.16.1). Wonders on public display in different parts of the ancient world included, in addition to the ubiquitous huge bones: the stone that Kronos had swallowed in place of the infant Zeus, the tusks of the Erymanthian Boar, the skeleton of the sea-monster to which Andromeda had been exposed, the hair of Medusa, the skin and the flute of Marsyas, samples of the clay from which Prometheus had fashioned the first humans, Orpheus' lyre, the spear with which Meleager slew the Calydonian boar, Achilleus's spear, Agamemnon's sceptre, the lance of Kaineus, a letter written by Sarpedon, the Golden Fleece, the wings used by Daidalos (Daedalus) to escape the Cretan labyrinth, the necklace of Eriphyle, and others. Probably few of these items were deliberate frauds and rather were rare or strange offerings to various gods that gradually became associated with legends of the heroic age (Rouse 318).

On the public display of material marvels in the ancient world see W.H.D. Rouse, *Greek Votive Offerings*, Cambridge 1902, 318–21; Ludwig Friedländer, 'What Interested Roman Tourists' and 'Exhibition of Natural Curiosities at Rome', in *Roman Life and Manners Under the Early Empire*, trans. A.B. Gough, London and New York 1913, 1: 367–94, 4: 6–11; Friedrich Pfister, *Der Reliquienkult im Altertum*, 2 vols, Gießen 1909–12; Garland 54–55. For the reblossoming of the tradition of displaying natural and cultural curiosities in the late Renaissance, see Oliver Impey and Arthur McGregor (eds), *The Origins of Museums: The Cabinets of Curiosities in Sixteenth- and Seventeenth-Century Europe*, Oxford 1985.

6

Commentary

Long-Lived Persons

The theme of the work is great longevity in humans. Phlegon's interest is not in rate of development, astonishingly slow as opposed to astonishingly fast lives (*Mir.* 32–33), but in the wonder of quantity.

I Persons Who Have Lived a Hundred Years

The headings accompanying the Roman numerals are Phlegon's, but the numerals have been supplied by modern editors.

Phlegon arranges persons first according to their age. He begins with centenarians and proceeds to older persons in spans of ten years at a time, although it is uncertain how far he continues this format because parts of his text are lost. Within age groups, he groups many persons together according to their first name.

from the census figures. Phlegon draws much of his data from the census for the Eighth Region of Italy, an area between the Apennines and the Po, the same region as Pliny (*NH* 7.49.162–64) surveys in his discussion of long life-spans. This census was made in AD 74 by Vespasian and his son Titus when they were censors. Male citizens were required to state under oath their full name, age, tribe or district of residence, the name of their father or patron, and a monetary valuation of their property. They also provided information about their wives and those children who were still subject to their authority (*in patria potestate*), but widows and orphans were listed on their own because they were not subject to a husband's or father's authority. See Kubitschek, 'Census', in *RE* 3: 1,914–24; Nicolet 48–88. Phlegon also includes persons from places outside of Italy: Macedonia, Pontos, Bithynia and Lusitania; see Theodor Mommsen, *Römisches Staatsrecht*, 3rd edn, Graz 1952, 2: 417 note 2.

1 **the town of Placentia.** Modern Piacenza. Among other towns mentioned by Phlegon, notice Ariminum (Rimini), Bononia (Bologna), Brixellum (Brescello), Faventia (Faenza), Regium (Reggio).

2 **Lucius Glaucius Verus, son of Lucius, of the town of Placentia.** This entry illustrates the usual format of the personal name of a free Roman male: Lucius = *praenomen*, the forename or given name; Glaucius = *nomen* (or *nomen gentilicium*), the name of the family, or *gens*, to which Lucius belongs, approximately our surname (on the form Glaucius, which is unparalleled, see Schulze 150, 357); Verus ('Truthful') = *cognomen*, or nickname, which in individual cases either is a personal nickname or indicates that its bearer belongs to a particular branch of the *gens*. There follows finally the father's *praenomen* and the subject's town of residence. The preceding entry, Lucius Cornelius, illustrates a male name consisting only of a *praenomen* and a *nomen*.

4 **Lucius Licinius Palus, freedman of Lucius, of the town of Placentia.** This name illustrates the usual format of the personal name of a freed male slave. The freedman takes the *praenomen* and *nomen* of his former master, in this case Lucius Licinius, to which his own name is appended as a *cognomen*.

11 town of Cornelia. Cornelia reappears in nos. 71, 72, 78, 91, 93. It is perhaps to be identified with the ancient Forum Cornelii, modern Imola.

15 . . . . Here and below, dots indicate places where words appear to have fallen out of the text.

17 Caesellius Cyrus. The lack of a patronymic or equivalent information suggests that the text is not sound here.

18 Catia, daughter of Gaius, of the town of Faventia. This entry, the first woman in the list, illustrates typical female nomenclature. Catia's name is a grammatically feminine form of her father's *nomen*, Catius. Females could also have *cognomina* or other distinguishing names, as in numbers 43–46, below.

19 Publius Fulvius Phryx, freedman of Lucius, of the town of Pollesia. A freedman who for some reason does not bear his former master's name. Phlegon's Pollesia is possibly the town of Pollentia.

20 Basileia. That is, 'Kingstown'; it reappears in no. 45. Basileia could be a Greek translation of Roman 'Regium'; so Heinrich Nissen, *Italische Landeskunde*, Berlin 1902, 2: 267 n. 4, although the town of Regium often appears as such in Phlegon's list (nos. 31, 36, 40, 41, 76, 90).

23 Aetosia. The reading appears to be corrupt.

25 Albius. Since the freedman Marcus seems to have two *nomina*, 'Terentius' and 'Albius', the second may be an error for a *cognomen* 'Albus' or 'Albinus' (Klein 135).

29 Nirellius. The name should probably be corrected to Nigellius (Klein 136, Morel 176).

32 Titus Veteranius . . . of the town of Bononia. Evidently a descendent of one of the Caesarian veterans who were settled at Bononia after the battle of Philippi in 41 BC; see Lawrence Keppie, *Colonisation and Veteran Settlement in Italy, 47–17 BC*, London 1983, 58–69, 187–88.

37 **Titus Aerusius Pollio.** For the 'Erusius' (ἐρούσιος) of the text, Jacoby prints Nauck's conjecture of 'Servius' (Σερούιος); I follow Schulze (344) in taking Erusius as representing Aerusius.

38 **Titus Camurius Tertius.** Phlegon's Kamorios (Καμόριος) doubtless renders Camurius; see Schulze 141.

39 **Turellia Forensis.** I adopt Klein's emendation of Turellia for the Turella of the text (Klein 135).

61 **Lucius Fidiclanius Nepos, Sinopian.** A member of an old Italian family; Cicero mentions Gaius Fidiculanius Falcula as a senator in the 70s BC (*Pro Caecina* 28, *Pro Cluentio* 103).

62 **Aloukios Apilioutas, from the town of Interamnesia.** 'Aloukios' appears in inscriptions as 'Aluquius'; see Klein 136, who also defends the manuscript reading 'Interamniesia' in preference to the emendation 'Interamnesia'. It presumably represents a Lusitanian town Interamna (or Interamnia or Interamnium).

66 **Conimbrigesia.** Presumably Conimbriga in western Hispania, the modern Coimbra, Portugal.

68 **Dokkourios.** Phlegon's Greek rendering of the name answers to the Latin inscriptional forms 'Docquirus' and 'Docquiricus' (Klein 136).

69 **Leledius.** A questionable form; see Klein 136.

70 **Potestas.** Klein's (136) emendation of Potesta.

72 **Cereonia.** Perhaps = Cervonia (Klein 137).

one hundred and one years. Phlegon sometimes spells out the numeral, as here, but more often gives it in numeric form; my translations reflect his practice.

II Persons who were registered as being from one hundred and one to one hundred and ten years

78 **Cocnania.** A garbled Latin name. Schulze (150) suggests Coculnia or Coclinia.

79 **Demokritos of Abdera, 104 years.** With this entry Phlegon begins integrating the names of a few prominent Greeks, drawing his information at first or second hand from Greek works. Pseudo-Lucian (*Mac.* 18) agrees that the philosopher lives till 104, but Diogenes Laertios (9.43) gives his age at death as 109.

80 **Ktesibios . . . as Apollodoros explains.** Apollodoros of Athens (*FGH* 244 F 49), author of a *Chronika*, known only in fragments. Cf. Pseudo-Lucian *Long-Lived Persons* 22.

81 **Hieronymos . . . as Agatharchides says.** Hieronymos of Kardia (*FGH* 154 T 2) and Agatharchides of Knidos (*FGH* 86 F 4). Cf. Pseudo-Lucian *Long-Lived Persons* 22.

83 **Publius Quisentius Ephyrion.** The χουισέντιος (*chouisentios*) of the manuscripts corresponds to no known Latin name, and editors emend to Κουισέντιος (Quisentius). Notice the attested forms Quisidius and Coesidius (Schulze 154, 168).

84 **Cottinas.** Schulze (78) mentions a modern place-name Cottignola near Faenze, which could be derived from the property of this man's family.

85 **Tannetana.** An unknown and presumably corrupt name.

III Persons registered as being from 110 to 120 years

91 **Purennius.** The text should probably be emended to
Perennius, which inscriptional evidence shows to have
been a widespread name in the Eighth Region of Italy;
see Morel 176.

93 **Lucius, [son] of Petrus.** Since Petrus is not a Roman
name, the text is probably corrupt.

Following Section III a section for persons 120–30 years of age
must have fallen out of the text. Drawing upon the same census
data, Pliny (*NH* 7.49.163–64) mentions persons 125 years old
from this region.

IV Persons registered as being from 130 to 140 years

96 **Terentius.** This man appears also in Pliny's list (*NH*
7.49.163).

97 **Faustus.** An instance of alleged autopsy, as in the case
of the androgyne Aitetos (*Mir.* 9).

V

After Section IV there has presumably dropped out of the text a
heading for persons 140–50 years of age.

98 **Arganthonios.** The poet Anakreon (fr. 361 Page) says
that he would not care to rule Tartessos for 150 years,
by which he must have in mind the reign, or perhaps
the life, of its long-lived ruler, Arganthonios. Herodotos
(1.163) says that King Arganthonios ruled the
Tartessians for eighty years and died after a life of
120 years. Phlegon, who attributes to Arganthonios a

life-time of 150 years on the authority of Anakreon and Herodotos, evidently did not consult the text of Herodotos directly. Indeed, since the long-lived Demokritos, Ktesibios, Hieronymos, and Arganthonios make an appearance both in Phlegon's *Long-Lived Persons* and also in Ps.-Lucian's work of the same name (10), it seems likely that the compilers draw their information from a third, anecdotal compilation on longevity that no longer survives; see Wachsmuth 1895:238.

Some information has fallen out of the text here. The biographer Diogenes Laertios remarks about Epimenides of Crete: 'He returned home and departed from life not long after, having lived a hundred and fifty seven years, as Phlegon says in his *Long-Lived Persons*' (*Lives of the Philosophers* 1.111 = FGH 257 F 38). Epimenides must have been found in Phlegon's work somewhere between the 150-year-old Arganthonios and the 1,000-year-old Sibyl. It seems safe to assume that other names and headings have been lost as well.

2 In the received text Phlegon moves from ordinary folk and a scattering of prominent Greeks to the Erythraean Sibyl and so to quasi-mythological tradition, just as in his *Book of Marvels* he intersperses recent events and mythological narratives. The presentation of the evidence for the age of the prophetess occupies the remainder of the document and consists mostly of oracular poetry, of which Phlegon is so fond.

99 **The Sibyl of Erythrai.** Many different Sibyls were distinguished in Phlegon's time, such as the Cumaean, Delphic and Erythraean. Varro is able to list ten (Lactantius *Div. Inst.* 1.6.8–12); on the proliferation of Sibyls see Potter 104–09.

just short of a thousand years. In support of this contention Phlegon presently gives excerpts from two oracles attributed to the Erythraean Sibyl, one in which the prophetess says she has lived for ten human life-spans, and another in which she declares 110 years as the maximum span of human life. On the tradition of the thousand-year life-span of the Sibyl, see Parke 20 note 15, Potter 116.

1 **But why.** The first of the two oracles. The mention of her age and her death occur in the first ten verses, and the remaining lines, which are not germane to the topic of longevity, are cited presumably for their own interest. On the structure of the oracle see Fontenrose 184.

2–5 **my own mad fate.** The Sibyl is represented as being possessed when she prophesies.

7 **At that time.** At what time? The phrase seems to allude to a future event that was mentioned earlier, before the beginning of our excerpt.

Leto's son. Apollo, whose divine provinces include prophecy.

11–22 **Whereupon my soul.** Upon her death the prophetess' body and soul mix with parts of the air and earth, infusing them with prophetic power and giving rise to three forms of divination: chance utterance, liver divination and bird divination; on forms of Greek divination see briefly Burkert 111–18. This prophetic narrative of the Sibyl's transformation probably is an original idea of the composer, who constructs it in the manner of a traditional aetiological story.

Plutarch was acquainted with this oracle and represents one of the interlocutors in a dialogue as summarizing its contents. From it we learn a strange detail that Phlegon omits: 'Sarapion recalled the verses in which she (the Sibyl) sang of herself, saying that not even after her death would she cease prophesying but would go round and round with the moon, having become the so-called face that appears on it' (*De Pythiae Oraculis, Mor.* 398c; cf. *Mor.* 566d). See further Parke 114–18, Potter 116–17.

13 omens woven together with shrewed riddling. The first new form of divination. This kind of omen, *kledon* (κληδών), means a chance utterance that a hearer takes to be significant and prophetic. For example, in Homer's *Odyssey* (18.112–17) the suitors unwittingly wish Odysseus victory over themselves when they say to a beggar, who really is the disguised Odysseus: 'Stranger, may Zeus and the other immortal gods grant you what you most wish for and is dearest to your heart'. Odysseus (says Homer) is delighted at the *kledon* (χαῖρεν δὲ κλεηδόνι).

17 in the withering of time. The expression (τερσαινομένοιο χρόνοιο 'as time dries up') is unusual, and since time cannot actually dry up, the text has been thought to be corrupt (Morel 176). But Phlegon employs a similar, if also unusual, expression (μαραινομένου τοῦ χρόνου) in a prose context (*Mir.* 15.2). The latter verb (μαραίνομαι 'waste, wither') is attested in ancient usage in connection with fire 'go out', a river 'dry up', a sound 'die away', wind 'abate' and other phenomena; Phlegon uses it of time in the sense that the life-span of the cosmos is 'running out'. The verb in the present passage (τερσαίνω 'dry up') is attested elsewhere of the desiccation of such things as blood, figs and flies, and so is more restricted in its range, covering a subset of the phenomena covered by μαραίνομαι, but the effective meaning of both verbs is essentially the same ('gradually diminish'), so that the text may be sound as it stands.

19 livers of grazing sheep. The second new kind of

divination. Professional interpreters divined the future from the form and colour of the liver of sheep.

21 **birds.** The third new form of divination. Interpreters inferred the future from the observed position and behaviour of birds.

By deriving liver divination, augury and *kledones* from herself, the Sibyl represents herself as the ultimate source of every kind of divination, both inspired and technical, or, as Cicero labels them in his *De Divinatione*, natural and artificial.

4 **life-span.** For other ancient speculations on the maximum life-span of human beings, which range from 112 to 124 years, see Pliny (*NH* 7.49.160). These estimates are close to the present observed upper-limit, which is 120 years of age; that is, no human being in modern times has been documented to have reached his or her 121st birthday (Young 11); however, this record has perhaps been broken by the celebrated Frenchwoman Jeanne Calment, who according to the newspapers celebrates her 121st birthday in February 1996.

Saecularia. That is, *Ludi Saeculares*, or 'Secular Games'.

The oracle is as follows. The second oracular fragment. Phlegon once again begins his excerpt with the verses that are relevant to his immediate point (vv. 1–2) and then continues beyond them, in this case quoting an additional thirty-six lines.

The oracular poem is found also in the account of the origin of the Secular Games given by the historian Zosimos (*Historia Nova* 2.1); see Diels 126–35 = *FGH* 257 F 40. It lacks the acrostic composition that appears in the Sibylline oracles in Chapter 10 of the *Book of Marvels* and that was anciently said to be characteristic of such oracles, although there may be a trace of it in verses 25–31, whose initial letters spell out ΔΑΠΕΔΟ (that is, most of the word δάπεδον = 'level surface'); if it is not a chance collocation, the oracle may be a newer composition that has incorporated older Sibylline verses (Diels 15).

On the oracle and the Secular Games see Diels 13–15; Nilsson, 'Saeculares ludi', in *RE* IA: 1,696–720; Lily Ross Taylor, 'New Light on the History of the Secular Games', *American Journal of Philology* 55 (1934) 101–20; Pighi; Adolf Kiessling, comm., *Q. Horatius Flaccus: Oden und Epoden*, 10. edn, (Berlin 1960) 466–70; den Boer 118–24; Doria 310–68; and Filippo Coarelli, 'Note sui *ludi Saeculares*', in *Spectacles Sportifs* 211–45.

2 **a hundred and ten years.** There is a subtext to the Sibyl's declaration of 110 years as the upper limit of human life. It defines a life-span as being up to a 110 years and so determines the interval between celebrations of the *Ludi Saeculares*, games celebrated once every *saeculum*, or 'age'; the festival should occur no more than once in any person's life-time. At first a *saeculum* was understood as a period of a hundred years, and the games were celebrated at intervals of about a century: in 348, 249, and either 149 or 146 BC (for various reasons there were no games in 49 or 46). Augustus's college of *quindecimviri*, however, accepted an interpretion according to which a *saeculum* was a 110 years, which, calculating from the games of the fourth century BC, provided a justification for the emperor holding the *Ludi Saeculares* in 17 BC. Notice Horace's 'sure cycle of ten times eleven years' in his hymn for Augustus's Secular Games (*Carmen Saeculare* 21–22). The appearance of this term as the upper limit of human life in the Sibyl's poem makes it likely that the oracle was composed during the reign of Augustus.

5 **on the field.** The Secular Games were celebrated at a sanctuary called the Terentum in the Campus Martius.

8 **Moirai.** The Fates. Horace addresses the *Parcae* 'Fates' in his hymn (*CS* 25–28).

9 **Eileithyia.** Goddess of childbirth. Horace invokes her as Ilithyia, Lucina and Genitalis (*CS* 13–24).

11 **Gaia.** Earth, when conceived as a living female (Latin *Tellus*). Cf. Horace *CS* 29–30.

13–14 **for to the Ouranian gods/Sacrifices are performed in daylight.** In Greek cultic practice a basic distinction was made between celestial gods (*ouranioi*) and gods of the earth (*chthonioi*); see Burkert 199–203. As Diels (15) points out, however, the expression is learned and pedantic.

16–17 **Phoibos Apollo,/Who is also called Helios.** More pedantry. The identification of Apollo and Helios is a sign of learned as opposed to popular tradition. Apollo and Sol both figure prominently in Horace's hymn (*CS* 1, 9–12, 33–34, 61–68, 75).

18–19 **Let Latin paeans/Sung by youths and maidens.** Horace's song (*CS* 6, 75–76) alludes to these lines, declaring that a Sibylline poem instructs a chorus of unblemished youths and maidens to sing a hymn to certain deities on this occasion.

21–22 Only those children may participate whose parents are both living, a common requirement in Greek as well as in Latin rites; notice Latin *patrimi* 'whose fathers are still alive' and *matrimi* 'whose mothers are still alive'. The participants must be ritually perfect.

25–26 **lustral agents.** Ordinarily the Greek word (λύματα) refers to the water used in ritual cleansing as well as to that which is washed off (e.g., dirt, blood), but here it renders Latin *suffimenta*, fumigants such as sulphur that were employed for ritual purification. Officials distributed *suffimenta* to celebrants before the *Ludi Saeculares* began; see Pighi 284–86.

28 **first fruits.** See the comment on *Mir.* 3.7.

31–32 Some words have dropped out of the text.

33–34 **During the following days/And nights.** Horace refers to celebrants thronging the festivities for three days and three nights (*CS* 22–24).

37–38 **all the earth of the Latins/Will always bear the yoke on its neck under your rule.** According to the Sibyl, the regular celebration of the Secular Games by the Romans will ensure their dominion over the Latins. The connection of the Secular Games and the maintenance of Roman rule over the Latins has been confirmed in this century by the discovery of fragments of the Severan *Acta* of the games, which include a prayer for the submission of the Latin allies (*utique semper Latinus obtemperassit*).

Phlegon of Tralleis. A so-called 'subscription', found in the manuscript at the end of Phlegon's work. For a discussion of its content see the Introduction.

7

Commentary

Olympiads

Fragment 1

This fragment, preserved in the same manuscript as that which contains the *Book of Marvels* and *Long-Lived Persons*, is an excerpt from Book One of Phlegon's *Olympiads*, describing the establishment of the Olympic Games.

Different versions of the founding of the Olympic Games have come down to us, varying in detail but broadly agreeing in presenting the establishment of the festival as occurring in three stages: first, sporadic athletic contests at Olympia; second, a period of neglect; and third, a revival of the festival and its establishment as a regular event. The principal ancient accounts are Pindar *Ol.* 10, Strabo 8.3.30 and 33, Pausanias 5 *passim*, Eusebios *Chron.* 1.190–94; translations are conveniently assembled in Robinson 32–55. See in general Christoph Ulf and Ingomar Weiler, 'Der Ursprung der antiken Olympischen Spiele in der Forschung: Versuch eines kritischen Kommentars', *Stadion* 6 (1980) 1–38, and on the present fragment Jacoby's commentary (*FGH* 257 F 1).

> 1 **Phlegon, freedman of the Emperor Hadrian: On the Olympic Games.** Phlegon's account of the founding of the Olympic Games was excerpted from Phlegon's larger work as a narrative of independent interest by someone who has supplied it with the present label.

Peisos, Pelops, . . . Herakles. Phlegon briefly alludes to the first two periods in the prehistory of the Games. During the first period Peisos, Pelops and Herakles were individual sponsors of notable contests at Olympia at the time when athletic games were held at irregular intervals at the site upon the invitation of this or that host, the contests often being funeral games held in honour of a recently deceased person. Olympia is located in the district of Elis in the Peloponnese.

the Peloponnesians left off the religious observance. An allusion to the second stage, the period of neglect, which according to Phlegon lasted about a century. Political strife arose in the Peloponnese but was not caused by the religious neglect of Olympia.

2 **Lykourgos . . . Iphitos . . . Kleosthenes.** The three founders of the Olympic Games as a regularly recurring festival, perhaps answering here to the three sporadic celebrants Peisos, Pelops and Herakles. They represent three lines of authority: a descendent of the hero Herakles (Lykourgos), an Elean (Iphitos) and a Pisatan (Kleosthenes). Although Olympia was located in Elis, the Eleans and Pisatans controlled the games at different times, each wresting it from the hands of the other. The two communities developed different versions of the establishment of the games, and their records of the winners in the individual contests sometimes disagreed.

without clothing. The Greeks told different stories of how the custom of nude athletic competition arose among them, but they agreed that in respect to unclothed athletics they differed from non-Greek peoples. For nudity in Greek athletics see Miller 17–20 (relevant texts in translation) and Myles McDonnel, 'Athletic Nudity among the Greeks and Etruscans: The

Evidence of the "Perizoma Vases"', in *Spectacles Sportifs* 395–407.

3 **the god.** That is, Apollo, via his oracle.

saying it would be better. This diction is standard Delphic for sanctioning an enterprise. A oracular consultant who has formed a plan of some sort seeks Apollo's blessing for the consultant's project, asking: 'Is it better and more good for me to do X?', and the god, if he approves, responds: 'It is better and more good for you to do X'. See Fontenrose 14–15 (response formula), 37–38 (query formula). For the oracle see Parke and Wormell 2: 197–98, nos 485–86; Fontenrose 268 (Q1–2).

4 **disc.** Since Phlegon alludes to the Olympic disc without further explanation, he must assume that it is familiar to his readers. The philosopher Aristotle (fourth century BC) and the travel-writer Pausanias (second century AD) each inspected the disc at Olympia, or at least a disc locally represented in their day as being the founding document of the festival (Plutarch *Lykourgos* 1.1, Pausanias 5.20.1); the object itself has not survived to our day. Reportedly it contained the names of Lykourgos and Iphitos as well as the terms of the armistice that the Eleans proclaimed on the occasion of each Olympic festival. The inscription ran circularly, following the shape of the copper disc. Other inscribed discs of various materials are known from antiquity, such as the famous Phaistos Disc from Crete with its spiral inscription; see Paul Jacobsthal, *Diskoi*, Archäologische Gesellschaft zu Berlin, Winckelmanns-programm 93, Berlin 1933.

Hellanodikai. The chief judges at the Olympic Games.

6 **The Pythia.** The priestess at Apollo's oracle at Delphi.

O dwellers. The oracle explains that Zeus has sent a plague upon the Peloponnesians because of their neglect of his festival, and that they can bring the plague to an end by renewing the festival. On the oracle see Parke and Wormell 2: 198, no. 487; Fontenrose 269 (Q3); and Gregory Nagy, *Pindar's Homer: The Lyric Possession of an Epic Past*, Baltimore 1990, 119–20.

The Pythia alludes to an earlier oracle in which Zeus revealed the rites of the Olympic festival, perhaps to Peisos, an incident that must belong to the story of the first period but is not recounted by Phlegon.

7 O dwellers. For the oracle see Parke and Wormell 2: 198, no. 488; Fontenrose 269 (Q4).

8 The founding of the Olympic Games, traditionally dated to 776 BC. The Homeric epics, probably composed in their present form in the eighth century BC, vividly attest to a contemporary enthusiasm for athletic competition among Greeks. Achilleus sponsors funeral games in honour of the slain Patroklos and awards prizes to the winners (*Iliad* 23.257–24.2), and King Alkinoos of the Phaiakians hosts after-dinner games in honour of his guest Odysseus (*Odyssey* 8.96–255). See Robinson 1–31, Harris 32–63, Miller 1–16.

9 Ministers of the Eleans. For the oracle see Parke and Wormell 2: 199, no. 489; Fontenrose 269 (Q5).

10 The subsequent history of the ancient Olympic Games as an institution involves the incorporation of new contests, the dropping of contests, and other kinds of change in response to the times; see Miller 203. The final chapters of Phlegon's narrative recount one famous innovation: how the practice of awarding garlands of wild olive to the winners came into being.

sixth (Olympiad). The first year of the sixth Olympiad was 756 BC.

chaplets. A chaplet was a fillet of wool wound around a branch (schol. vet. on Sophokles *Oedipus Rex* 3: στέμμα δέ ἐστι τὸ προσειλημένον ἔριον τῶι θαλλῶι); see further Jean Bollack, *L'Oedipe roi de Sophocle: Le texte et ses interpretations,* Lille 1990, 2: 6–8.

the produce of sheep. For the oracle see Parke and Wormell 2: 199–200, nos 490–91; Fontenrose 269–70 (Q6). The (unintentionally) ambiguous phrase (μήλειον καρπόν) could refer to the 'produce' either of *apple trees* or of *sheep,* and scholars commonly understand the oracle to forbid a use of 'apple trees'. But probably the oracle distinguishes, not apple trees from olive trees as sources of garlands, but chaplets fashioned of olive branches and wrapped with wool from garlands made of olive branches alone. Besides, if the phrase 'produce of apple-trees' were correct, it would more naturally signify 'apples' than 'apple branches', which would make no sense as a material from which to fashion garlands.

11 **stadium race.** The Greek *stadion* (στάδιον) was 600 feet long, but inasmuch as each *stadion* was laid out according to actual human feet and not according to a standard unit of measure, particular *stadia* varied with one another in their length. The *stadion* at Olympia measures 192.27 meters; see Finley and Pleket xiii. The winner of the stadium race is mentioned because this contest was the most famous of the Games, and a particular Olympiad was known by the winner of the stadium race.

eighth Olympiad. 752 BC.

Fragment 12

Another sizable fragment, this one dealing with the 177th Olympiad (72–69 BC), is preserved in a work of the Byzantine scholar Photios (*Bibl.* 97), who says that he has read the first five books of Phlegon's *Olympiads*, up to the 177th Olympiad, and recounts data for that Olympiad. See Jacoby's commentary (*FGH* 257 F 12).

2 **Hypsikles . . . long course.** In distance all foot-races were multiples of *stadia*. The long course (δόλιχος) apparently varied in length at different athletic sites but seems to have been twenty *stadia* at Olympia; see Harris 65 and 73. Runners ran, not on an oval-shaped course, but on the linear *stadion*, which had a turning post at each end so that in the long course the contestants made a full turn around the further post and returned again on the straight track, repeating this procedure until they had run the specified distance.

Gaius of Rome: long course. The listing of a second winner for the same event, and a Roman at that, is puzzling.

Aristonymidas . . . pentathlon. The pentathlon consisted of five events: the long jump, discus, javelin, foot race and wrestling; see Harris 77–80.

Isidoros . . . wrestling, not thrown in the Circuit. The Greeks referred to the stretch of time embraced by the four great public games—Olympic, Nemean, Pythian, and Isthmian—as a Circuit (περίοδος). Isidoros entered the wrestling event in all four panhellenic games, wherein no opponent was able to throw him.

Atyanas . . . boxing. Although the text is corrupt, this seems to be its sense. It is uncertain why the name of Atyanas's father is listed, since Phlegon does not usually record this information for victors. In a speech Cicero mentions Atyanas as a man of noble birth who was killed by pirates and whose name is familiar to most of Cicero's audience, since (he says) Atyanas was a victor at Olympia in boxing, an honour that is almost greater among Greeks than the celebration of a triumph is among Romans (*Pro Flacco* 13.31).

Sphodrias . . . pankration. The pankration was a combat sport that involved a mixture of wrestling and boxing; see Harris 105–09.

Sosigenes . . . boys' stadium race. Boys between twelve and seventeen years of age were eligible for the boys' events; see Finley and Pleket 35.

Hekatomnos . . . double course, and hoplite race. The double course (δίαυλος 'double flute') was a race two *stadia* in length, that is, approximately 400 yards; and the hoplite event was a race of the same distance in which the runners wore armour. See Harris 74–75.

four-horse chariot. Races involving horses took place on the hippodrome, an open space located near the stadium. The credit for the victory went primarily to the animals and their owners and only secondarily to the jockeys, whose names are not recorded. See Finley and Pleket 27–32.

With no transition, at least as Photios reports it, the catalogue of victors ends and that of other events occurring during the Olympiad begins. The parallelism between men striving in games and men striving in wars, some winning and some losing, is striking today in a way that presumably it was not to the ancients.

3 **Lucullus was besieging Amisos.** The siege of the Greek city of Amisos on the southern coast of the Euxine Sea, begun in 72 BC, was an incident in the Third

Mithridatic War between Rome and King Mithridates VI of Pontos. The Roman effort was led by the proconsul Lucius Licinius Lucullus (subject of a biography by Plutarch in his *Parallel Lives*). The other two commanders, L. Licinius Murena (defendant in Cicero's speech *Pro Murena*) and M. Fabius Hadrianus, were legates, or lieutenants, under Lucullus.

5 **many other things happened.** We should expect four groups of events answering to the four years of the Olympiad, whereas what we find is one unlabelled cluster followed by a group for the third year and a group for the fourth year. It appears that for some reason Photios has combined some events of the first two years of the Olympiad and passed over others with the present dismissive statement. Whether he follows Phlegon closely elsewhere or abbreviates the text is uncertain.

6 **In the third year of the Olympiad.** 70 BC.

910,000 Romans were enrolled. The figure is the number of adult male citizens counted in the Roman census of 70 BC; see Livy *Per.* 98 and Nicolet 48. Cicero remarks on the great crowds who came to Rome that year from all over Italy to be present at the elections, games, and census (I *Verr.* 1.18.54).

8 **Patron succeeded Phaidros the Epicurean.** At the death of the Athenian philosopher Phaidros (*c*138–70 BC), Patron became head of the Epicurean school at Athens. Atticus and Cicero were acquainted with Phaidros and thought kindly of him (Cicero *De Finibus* 1.5.16, *De Legibus* 1.20.53); see A.E. Raubitschek, 'Phaidros and his Roman Pupils', *Hesperia* 18 (1949) 98–103. Very little is known of Patron.

9 **The poet Vergilius Maro.** Virgil was born on October 15th.

10 **In the fourth year.** 69 BC.

Tigranes. Continuing his aggression (Section 3, above), Lucullus invaded Armenia and routed the forces of Mithridates's ally, King Tigranes.

11 **Catulus consecrated the Capitol.** The temple of Jupiter on the Capitoline was consecrated by Quintus Catulus after it had been destroyed by fire and rebuilt (Livy *Per.* 98).

12 **Metellus.** Quintus Caecilius Metellus Creticus, consul in 69, was given the command against the infamous pirates in Crete. He was successful, besieging and capturing many Cretan towns.

13 **The pirate Athenodoros.** In the long history of piracy in the Mediterranean, the years around 69 ranked among the worst. Among other depredations, the small but prosperous island of Delos, a centre of the ancient slave trade, was attacked by pirates and utterly destroyed. Gaius Valerius Triarius, a legate under the command of Lucullus, build a fortification wall for protection in the future, but the island never recovered. See Henry A. Ormerod, *Piracy in the Ancient World*, Liverpool and London 1924, 232–33; Lionel Casson, *The Ancient Mariners*, 2nd edn, Princeton 1991, 165–69.

the so-called gods. In reporting Phlegon's work the Byzantine scholar Photios piously inserts the adjective 'so-called' to apply to the non-Christian gods.

Appendix 1

Persons Who Died and Returned to Life

Naumachios the Epirote, a man who lived in our grandfathers' time, reports that Polykritos the Aitolian, the most distinguished of the Aitolians and an Aitolarch, died and returned to life in the ninth month after his death. He showed up at the general assembly of the Aitolians where he gave them excellent advice concerning the matters they were deliberating. Hieron the Ephesian and other historians witnessed these events and wrote about them to King Antigonos and to other friends of theirs who were elsewhere.

And not only Polykritos but also a certain man by the name of Eurynous had the same experience not long before in Nikopolis. Buried before the city by his relatives he returned to life following the fifteenth day of his burial, saying that he had seen and heard many marvellous things beneath the earth but that he had been forbidden to divulge any of it. He lived for a long time after this and was perceived to be a more upright person after his return to life than before.

To these he adds a third person, born only yesterday, as they say, Rufus of Philippi in Macedonia, a man who had been deemed worthy of the most important high-priesthood in Thessalonica. He died and returned to life on the third day, and when he returned to life he said that he had been sent back by the chthonic gods to discharge to the people an account of the sights he had experienced. He lived until he had fulfilled this charge and then died again.

The case *par excellence* is Philinnion, during the reign of Philip. The daughter of the Amphipolitans Demostratos and Charito, she died as a newly-wed. Her husband had been Krateros. In the sixth month after her death she returned to life and for many nights in a row secretly consorted with a young man, Machates, because of her love for him. He had come to Demostratos from his native city of Pella. She was detected and died again after proclaiming that what she had done was done in accord with the will of the subterranean deities. Her corpse was seen by everyone as it lay in state in her father's house. In their disbelief at what had happened the members of her family went to the place that had earlier received her body, dug the place up, and found it to be empty. The events are described in a number of letters, some written by Hipparchos and some written by Arrhidaios (who was in charge of Amphipolis) to Philip.

Proklos Diadochos *In Platonis Rem Publicam Commentarii* II, pp. 115–16 Kroll. See *Book of Marvels*, Chapters 1–2.

Appendix 2

The Bride of Corinth

by Johann Wolfgang Goethe
translated by Breon Mitchell

From Athens to Corinth a youth did come,
A stranger there to everyone.
He hoped to join those citizens;
Two fathers who were longtime friends,
Had pledged each other,
Their son and daughter,
As man and bride while both were young.

But would he find a welcome here,
Unless the price he paid were dear?
For he was heathen in his family life,
While they were baptized in the name of Christ.
When the blossom of belief is new,
Both love and pledges to be true,
Are often seen as weeds of strife.

And all at home were quiet and still,
Father, daughter, only mother up that night.
She welcomes him with all good will,

And leads him to a hall of light.
Food and wine are brought to him,
Before he thinks to ask for them:
And having served her guest she bids good night.

But though the food is well prepared,
He is not moved to drink or eat;
Too tired to take of wine or meat,
He throws himself still dressed upon the bed,
And is nearly fast asleep,
When a strange visitor does creep,
Through unlocked door into his suite.

Now he sees by the lamp's dim glow,
A white dress and veil which flow
Into his room; a chaste and modest maid,
A black and golden band upon her forehead laid.
And catching sight
of him, she starts in fright,
And lifts white hand in shock, dismayed.

'Am I,' she cries, 'so little known at home,
That no one tells me guests have come?
So thus they keep me in my cell!
And now they shame me too, as well.
Don't rise, but rest instead,
Within the comfort of your bed,
And I'll return from whence I've come.'

'Stay, beauteous maid!' the boy appealed,
And leapt from bed with movement swift,
'Here is Ceres', here is Bacchus' gift;
And you add that of love, sweet child!
You're pale with fright!
Dear heart, let's spend the night,
And see the pleasure of the gods revealed.'

'Stay, young man, stand fast!
I have no part in pleasures now.
The final step, alas, is long since past,
Due to my sick mother's folly vast,
Who in recovering made a vow,
That youth and nature henceforth must bow
Their heads to heaven's will at last.

And so the ancient gods' bright throng,
Did leave our silent house ere long.
Just One, invisible, now reigned on high,
Whose precious Son upon the cross did die;
No sacrifices here
Of lamb or steer,
But human sacrifice where none belong.'

He ponders well and weighs each word,
Not one of which has gone unheard.
Can it be in this quiet place,
I see at last my bride's dear face?
'You must be mine!
For blessings divine,
Were granted by your father's grace.'

'You won't have me for your own, good soul!
My younger sister's chosen for that role.
While I lie in anguish in my cell,
Ah, in her arms please think of me as well,
Who only thinks of you,
Who dies of love that's true,
Soon sleeping 'neath the earth as bells do toll.'

'No! By this flame our fathers swore,
It lights our way to Hymen's door;
You are not lost to love or me,
In Father's house we soon shall be.

My love, but wait!
Let's celebrate
This wedding feast immediately.'

And now they pass to one another, as of old,
Tokens of their faith; she to him a chain of gold,
And he to her a cup beyond compare,
Of silver wrought, a work of art most fair.
'Much too fine for me;
I ask instead of thee,
A simpler gift, a lock of hair.'

The bell announced the witching hour of night,
And now at last she seemed all right.
With pale and eager lips she sipped the wine,
Pressed dark and blood-like from the vine.
Yet when he passed the bread,
She simply shook her head,
And would not take a single bite.

And then the cup passed to the youth,
Who drank the wine as eagerly.
Begging for love, sipping silently;
His poor heart sick with love in truth,
Continued to insist,
She continued to resist,
Till he fell weeping on his bed in bitter ruth.

And she throws herself beside him.
'Ah, how it hurts to see you in pain!
But, oh, if you but touched a single limb,
You'd shudder at that which I conceal in vain.
As white as snow,
But icy cold,
Is the loved one you now seek to gain.'

Strongly he wraps her in his arms,
Invigorated by the youthful power of love:
'I bring to you a strength that warms,
Even if t'were from the grave you come!
Breath on breath, and kiss on kiss!
Overflow of love and bliss!
Burn you not, and feel me burn as one?'

Love presses them firmly to each other,
And tears are mingled with their passion's breath;
Eagerly she draws from her lover,
His mouth in flame, each knows the other best.
The frenzy of his love,
Warms her languid blood,
And yet no heart does beat within her breast.

Anon, her mother climbs the stairs,
Quietly, intent on night affairs.
Stops at the door, then listens more closely,
Wondering what those sounds might be.
Tones of lament and passion's pride,
The bridegroom and his blissful bride,
The stammering signs of lovers' frenzy.

Motionless she waits outside the door,
Because she wants to know for sure.
And she hears the oaths of love outpour;
Sweet words and flattery she must endure:
'Shh! Here's morning's light!'—
'But then again tomorrow night,
I'll see you here?' — and kiss on kiss once more.

Now the mother's rage at last turns wild,
She quickly picks the lock, which she knows best:
'Must I live to see our home defiled
By whores who give themselves to any guest?'

And so goes in.
By lamplight dim,
She sees—Oh god! She sees her eldest child.

And the youth, as shocked as he can be,
Attempts to cover his beloved with her veil
And with a tapestry, to no avail;
She twists and turns until she's free.
With a spirit's power,
She rises, will not cower,
Sits up in bed, sits there quietly.

'Mother! Mother!' she speaks with hollow sound,
'You'd deny me this one blissful night!
And drive me forth from warmth I've found.
Am I awakened only to despair and fright?
Can you be not simply proud,
You wrapped me in an early shroud,
And buried me deep within the ground?

But from the confines of the earth, of late,
A different court has called me forth.
The droning hymns of priests have little worth,
And their blessings carry little weight.
Neither salt nor water cool
What young ones feel;
Ah, the very earth dampens not a love this great.

This youth you see was promised me,
When the bright temple of Venus still did stand.
Mother, you broke the word you gave when free,
Because a false oath held you in its band!
Yet no god will allow
A mother to break a solemn vow,
She's made to give her daughter's hand.

I was driven from my early grave, you see,
To seek that which was mine by right,
To love a man now lost to me,
To suck the blood of his heart by night.
And when I'm done,
To find another one
Among the young to feel the fury of my might.

Handsome youth! No longer can you live;
In this place you now must pine away.
Keep the golden chain that I did give;
I'll take your lock of hair this day.
Look closely, it shan't remain that way,
For tomorrow you'll be gray,
And only brown may you return to stay.

Now listen, Mother, to my final plea:
Stack a mighty pile of wood for him and me,
Open up my dreary little cell!
Let two lovers die in flames, and rest as well!
While the sparks still fly,
As the glowing ashes die,
We'll hurry to the ancient gods on high.'

See *Book of Marvels*, Chapter 1.

Appendix 3

Achilleus' Ghost and the Trojan Maiden

It is said that Achilleus once appeared in person to a merchant who frequented his island. Achilleus recounted what happened at Troy, entertained him with drink, and asked him to sail over to Ilion and bring a Trojan maiden back to him, describing such and such a girl who was such and such a person's slave in Ilion. Surprised at the request, the stranger made bold to inquire why he wanted a Trojan slave. Achilleus said: 'Stranger, because she was born in the very place that Hektor and those before Hektor were born, and is a female descendant of the line of Priam and Dardanos.'

Now the merchant, thinking that Achilleus loved the girl, purchased her and sailed back to the island, where Achilleus thanked him upon his arrival and instructed him to keep the girl aboard his ship because, I think, the island was not accessible to women, and to come to his shrine in the evening to dine with him and Helen. When the merchant arrived, Achilleus gave him a great deal of money, which merchants are unable to resist, and said he was making the man his guest-friend, rendering his commerce prosperous, and causing his ship to have a good voyage. At daybreak he said: 'Take these things and sail, and leave the girl for me on the beach.' But the merchant and his crew

were not yet a stade away from land when the girl's cries
assaulted their ears, for Achilleus was mangling her and tearing
her apart limb from limb.

Philostratos *Heroikos* 215. See *Book of Marvels*, Chapter 2.

Index